YOU'RE GOING TO BE A DAD: A PREGNANCY GUIDE FOR MEN

THE ESSENTIAL FIRST-TIME DAD'S SURVIVAL
GUIDE: TIPS FOR BECOMING A NEW FATHER,
BEING PREPARED IN THE WHOLE NINE MONTHS,
THE FIRST YEAR, AND BEYOND

Timothy Barnet

TABLE OF CONTENTS

1

THE CHALLENGE OF PREGNANCY FOR A MODERN DAD

You may have heard a lot about fatherhood. Some of what you've heard might be good, and some might terrify you. You may hear all kinds of anecdotal stories from fathers around the block or those in your friend group, only to be left horrified and concerned about the stress of it all. You may even hear a lot of positive stories about spelling bees and first steps, but these are easily overshadowed by doctors' visits and existential questions like *"how do I make sure that my child is a good person?"*

The truth of fatherhood is that it's a different journey for each man. No two fathers will have the same experience, and a lot of that experience depends on the family dynamic, the child, and you, the father. However, no matter what personality type, it's important to go into fatherhood knowing some basic ground rules from conception to birth.

There is one universal truth about pregnancy that affects everyone: your life is about to change. This book is meant to offer you guidance, information, and advice for getting through everything from the moment of conception to the moment you hold your child in your arms for the first time.

Deciding on Pregnancy - A Shared Choice

Deciding and planning to conceive a child is no easy choice. This decision may have come with many discussions and dreams about the future over countless dinners. In these talks, you and your partner may have conjured up images of walking through the neighborhood in October, leaves crunchy under your child's feet as they giggle into the evening air. The decision to conceive a child tends to have a similar vision—one in which you and your partner lovingly adore the child you made together.

The decision to have a child ultimately entails a lot of responsibility. This much of what you have heard is true. Fatherhood is a lifelong journey full of responsibility and difficulty. Deciding to have a child means signing yourself up for many experiences that may make you stop and grit your teeth to avoid saying some choice words. If you have rambunctious children, you may be looking at broken bones and shattered windows from wayward baseballs. However, these difficult experiences come with many purely perfect experiences, like your first game of catch with your child in the park. Watching your child fall in love with the same hobbies as yourself or your partner can invoke feelings of joy, excitement, and wonder how you and your spouse managed to raise someone so perfect. Even the littlest moments, like watching them get engrossed in a movie or hearing them sound out the words on the Amazon Prime truck, can feel like you've been knocked off your feet all over again.

Fatherhood is a mountain climb, not a hike. There will be moments in which you feel like you're carrying the weight of your child's world on your shoulders—and, sometimes, you will literally be carrying their entire weight on your shoulders, yes. Yet, you'll be satisfied to do so. In many cases, you will *want* to be wanted for your child's needs.

The responsibilities you both saw may have been hard, filled with sleepless nights and diaper changes from hell, but they may make you smile when you think about it. These frustrating moments will go into the chronicles of your child's life, something that you bring up time and again to remind them of the hard work you did for them and the love you have for their existence.

You may feel like your future is incomplete without this little version of you and your partner to hold in your arms and dote upon. Little trinkets or TV show ads might catch your attention and make you long for a little hand to slip into yours and warm your chest from the inside out. There is nothing quite like the unconditional love that a child has for their father. Perhaps that is the love you yearn for—turning the love that you and your partner share into a love that is the basis for a whole family unit and is nearly magical and unbreakable.

Caring For Yourself

Taking care of your physical and mental health is of the utmost importance at any point in your life, but especially when a child is on the way. During the first few months of your child's life, there will be disrupted routines, sleepless nights, and what can feel like utter chaos. This doesn't mean you will fall apart and lose yourself. Instead, you'll need to foster emotional and physical resilience to the challenges that arise.

During pregnancy, your partner may struggle with sleep, which might disrupt your sleep. Between the sparked anxiety from her lack of rest and the potentially increased nighttime movements from her side of the bed, you might find yourself running low on rest. In these cases, get extra sleep. This kind of care for yourself is vital to your daily functioning. Even a 30-minute nap can help rejuvenate you and make you more emotionally resilient to outside stressors.

What your version of self-care looks like doesn't matter. The only thing that matters is that you engage in it to assist with the challenges of your life and keep yourself at the top of your game for the journey ahead—however awesome and daunting it proves to be.

 Tips for new dads

When you find the bottle notice, stop and read the chapter tip. You will find useful tips every month!

What It Means To Be a Father

I won't lie to you: being a father in the modern era is hard. It means making the ultimate sacrifices of your time, your energy, and your quiet time. Balancing quality time with your children and partner on top of work constraints and other obligations can feel overwhelming. It might even invoke stress responses like shaking palms, clenching your teeth, and struggling to maintain a normal heart rate. It's important to pause and remember that above all else, you are a valued and loved member of your family, just like your partner. You'd likely hate for the mother of your children to feel as stressed as you might feel. Take a moment and breathe. Your obligations as a father might be many and heavy, but they are not without reward.

Fatherhood comes with the ultimate payday: the warmth, the love, and the lifelong connection with the child you raise. The closer connection with your spouse as you work together to foster a loving environment for your family is an added bonus. Fatherhood is described best by blogger Siied Brown, who says, "being a father means being loyal, honest, and strong no matter if times are good or bad. It's setting an example and also being everything your child needs you to be, whenever they need it. It's the most important duty a man can hold" (2020). But part of becoming a father means understanding pregnancy from the moment it begins to the moment your child is warm against your chest.

That being said, this survival guide is here to help. Within these pages, you'll discover the progression of pregnancy and its effects on your partner's body. You'll also learn the importance of planning out your future and a routine to ensure your own health and mental care are accounted for. While also discovering how best to take care of your partner during this transition period, you'll follow up with your baby's size and shape and realize how incredibly small your child is.

Financial planning is an absolute must—I cannot stress it enough. Children are notoriously expensive, but these nine months will give you more than enough time to sit down with your partner and discuss how you can work together to figure out the best ways to offer your child the healthcare and basic necessities they require. This means accounting for formula, diapers, baby wipes, and clothing they inevitably grow out of in only a few months.

There's a lot to consider when thinking about friends and family, as well. How do you want to handle the sudden influx of visitors in the months of gestation? Surely, many of your relatives—and your partner's—will be excited about the new addition to your family, and that can be a tad overwhelming for some couples. Especially fathers, as they can often feel out of their depth with nothing to actually do yet since the baby is still *in utero*.

Another huge step that you'll learn more about is the discovery of your child's gender and how to navigate the nerves that may arise upon finding out. From there, you'll learn how to take care of yourself while also giving your partner the attention she requires while carrying your child. This is a delicate balance, but one you can maneuver with grace and proper communication.

We'll discuss sex during pregnancy as it can cause many people to feel uncomfortable, but in truth, the concern is not entirely warranted. You'll then learn about what to pack in your hospital bag and the possible complications that can arise at around the seventh month of gestation.

At around month eight, you and your partner will likely want to set up a nursery and attend prenatal classes, which can be boring at first. However, you will gain a wealth of information from these courses. Although nothing could prepare you for the culmination of this nine-month journey, we will discuss the typical progress of birth and what usually happens during that process.

Finally, you'll learn all about how your life will change, how to hold your baby, change a diaper, and interact with the newest member of your family. From going outside to sharing your favorite foods with your child, there are many new experiences ahead.

2

THE FIRST TRIMESTER - MONTH ONE

The beginning of pregnancy is the perfect time to start planning. It's never too early to think about your family, your future, and your goals. The pregnancy preparations can be overwhelming, especially for guys who don't have to form a whole human being inside them, but there is plenty that the male can do. One of the most vitally important aspects during this time is making sure that your mental and physical health is in order. First, take a deep breath and realize that pregnancy is a whole nine months. There is plenty of time to get things together and make a plan that works well for you, your spouse, and your future family.

Preparing for Pregnancy

Some men don't get the luxury of preparing for the pregnancy before it happens. If you are one of those lucky men who get the head start of knowing a baby is coming before the actual conception, you're already ahead of the curve. Having this opportunity can be an awesome way to get ahead of some hurdles—like finding the perfect glider for your wife to rest in or investing in the perfect financial plan for your child's future education.

However, the most important thing to prepare for is how pregnancy works.

Conception

Certain hurdles that require the intervention of modern medicine can affect the decision to conceive a child. Fertility issues are common; around ten percent of women in the United States alone struggle with getting pregnant ("Infertility," n.d.). In cases where it is difficult to get pregnant, it's important to keep calm and seek professional medical care to pursue options for your family.

When your partner comes out of the bathroom with the pregnancy test in hand, you might get the urge to cry, scream for joy, or start jumping for literal joy. Chances are, your partner will meet any sign of joy with absolute adoration. Remember that crying is not a bad thing. You're allowed to express your emotions however you feel most appropriate. There may be a complicated array of emotions going through your brain: happiness, joy, fear, confusion, and even regret. While many people won't discuss the negative emotions they may feel when their partner gets pregnant, it's important to note that these emotions are normal. Let them exist while also reassuring yourself that these normal emotions will go away in time. The unknown is terrifying, and you are embarking on a journey into it. Let yourself have emotions as you continue the path.

You might be at a loss for words or find yourself rambling. Some things would be ideal to say when you find out you're going to be a father, while you should avoid saying other things. Some good things to say are:

- "I'm going to be a father." Straight-up telling the truth of the matter can make it more real for you and help you process the reality of the moment.
- Any type of excited exclamation, laugh or cry.

- Asking how your partner is feeling and if they're okay.
- "What do we do now?" Some people may view this question as bad, but it can convey a sense of calmness and control to your partner. This can instill confidence and security in you both.

That being said, here are some things to avoid saying:

- Anything resembling the words "oh no," "oh crap," or an expletive that expresses regret.
- "I hope it's a boy." Just, not cool. That's a lot of pressure for a pregnant woman.
- "I can't do this." It's okay to have emotions, but now may not be the best time to express any type of negative sentiment.

The first month may not be easy, but you and your partner can get through planning, fears, and wellness checks as a team. What you can expect from your partner is excitement, planning, and probably a hundred discussions on baby names, outfits, and visions of the future.

Planning For the Future

During the first month, your main priority as the father of the growing child is to take care of your spouse. This means checking on their emotional and physical well-being and putting in a little more effort around the house. One side-effect of pregnancy in the first month is extreme fatigue, so your partner may not be keen to pull out the vacuum or go food shopping. Everyday tasks may occasionally fall to you as she builds her stamina during the pregnancy. Besides some financial planning and online browsing for cribs and baby carriers, consider making your partner some healthy meals, practicing meditations that help keep you both calm, and taking care of all heavy lifting around the home.

You and your partner may want to consider antenatal classes, which can help you learn practical things about pregnancy, labor, and birth before the baby comes ("First Trimester," 2017). These classes will discuss the next steps in pregnancy, how to prepare for the delivery of your baby, the signs of labor, and the different stages of labor. These classes can also provide alternative perspectives about birthing positions and how to relax and breathe during stressful moments in the pregnancy ("Antenatal Classes," 2019). Some of these classes are specifically led by and made for fathers for the sole purpose of helping fathers learn the ropes of pregnancy and what they can do to help their partner through the process. Consider finding one in your local area or online.

Here are some of the other dos and don'ts of the coming month:

Do:

- Talk with your partner about everything that you both are feeling. It's an intense time, and emotions may be running high for both of you. You both need to maintain a close bond and share your emotions, dreams, and visions of the future. Communication with your partner has never been more important than during pregnancy, and exploring problems together through clear and open dialog can make both feel better about the road ahead.

- Learn about the restrictions associated with pregnancy. Your partner will not be able to eat a variety of foods like uncooked or raw foods, hot dogs, some lunch meats, seafood, alcohol, and anything unpasteurized ("First 20 Things," 2019).
- Figure out the progression of pregnancy, what happens in each trimester, and how the baby develops. This guide will give you vital information about a standard pregnancy. You'll also want to learn the terms associated with pregnancy, such as prenatal, ultrasound, sonogram, and contraction.
- Break free from bad health habits and seek mental health habits. If you're a chronic smoker, a more-than-average drinker, or someone prone to anxiety, you'll want to get the necessary help to resolve these challenges before your baby arrives.
- Prepare for the way your life and relationship will change. Your partner's body will change, your relationship together will change, and the role you play in each other's lives will morph. Seeking out information, testimonials, and other information on how those changes happen will help you gear up to prevent issues that may arise from the coming obstacles of sleepless nights.

Don't:

- Wait until the pregnancy has progressed to start researching. The best time to look into more information about health and wellness is right now. You'll want to know how your baby grows and develops, and waiting will only keep you in the dark.

- Wait to start a financial plan for your family. You have plenty of time to figure out your financial life if you start planning now. However, waiting will put you into a hole that may be hard to dig out of if you haven't accounted for diapers, formula, and other baby-related expenses.
- Sacrifice your alone time and self-care needs. Just like your partner needs rest and relaxation, so do you.
- Focus on the negatives or major changes that you're scared of. Your life is going to change, but those changes will come with both good and bad aspects. Now is the time to celebrate all the experiences that lie in your future and prepare for the things that you can foresee while accepting that some things will be out of your hands.
- Blurt out the news to friends and family. This can be a monumental moment for your partner—ya know, the one carrying your baby—and you wouldn't want to disrespect her wishes if she wants to refrain from sharing too soon. Some couples decide to wait to share their news until the first trimester ends because 80 percent of miscarriages occur during the first trimester (Marcin, 2018). Instead, talk with your partner about what you would both prefer regarding announcing the pregnancy.

Mental Health and Physical Wellness

Nothing can get you into a doctor's office faster than finding out you have a child on the way. Getting an overall physical done can help give you an idea of any underlying conditions you may have and help you overcome any moderate health issues. High blood work, anxiety, or depression are incredibly common and should be handled by a medical professional as soon as possible—especially with the oncoming responsibilities of pregnancy.

The best way to keep your mental health in check is to make sure you're getting plenty of downtime to experience peace, quiet, and engage in hobbies. Doing something you love and getting plenty of rest helps you create a wall of emotional resilience that will prove useful for when your child arrives.

Physical fitness is also key to maintaining health and wellness. Engage in regular physical exercise and eat healthy meals full of minerals and vitamins. Starting a regimen of multivitamins and supplements couldn't hurt, either.

Your partner will be no stranger to doctor's offices for the next few months, either. Consider helping her with visits to the general practitioner, midwife, or obstetrician. In the first month, she may not need much help getting there unless morning sickness or motion sickness is particularly terrible, but the emotional support can create a closer bond between you that will be invaluable as the pregnancy progresses.

Baby Development: Month One

One of the first tests makes sure your partner is actually pregnant. Home tests can be inaccurate, but a urine sample will look at the HCG levels in her body and confirm that there really is a baby growing in the womb.

During the first month of your baby's development, they are still just an egg burrowing into the lining of their mother's womb. Within the first four weeks, the egg develops three layers. One layer is for developing their breathing and digestive systems; one is for the heart and blood vessels; the last layer composes the brain and nervous system. These changes are the culprits for many of the pregnancy-related symptoms like fatigue, cramping, and spotting.

Tip #1: Reach Out to Other Dads

Finding out you're going to be a father mixed with the whirlwind of life that comes from the first month of pregnancy can make you feel like you've just run a marathon and need to pause and catch your breath. When in doubt, consider reaching out to another father you know and get their advice on what you can do to help your partner, plan for the future, and focus on keeping yourself and your family healthy. Guys, much like anyone, will want to give you the low-down on their experiences—both the good and bad. Doing this as soon as you're comfortable discussing your partner's pregnancy can help you figure out which real-life practices you can implement to build a good foundation for your whole family.

3

THE FIRST TRIMESTER - MONTH TWO

The first month is over! Breathe a sigh of relief and congratulate yourself on getting through the first step in the process. You have likely made many changes in your life, from prioritizing to taking care of your partner. In this chapter, we'll be discussing the second month of pregnancy and what you can do to work with your partner to foster a safe and healthy environment for your family. We will also discuss the progression of your child's development and any special tests and exams that will be happening during this second month.

Early Pregnancy Symptoms

In the last chapter, we discussed the most common pregnancy symptoms that begin in the first trimester. Each woman is different; some women won't experience these symptoms until the second month, while others may experience these symptoms within the first few weeks of pregnancy (Holland, 2021). When the baby gets a little bigger, and their presence is more noticeable, the pregnancy symptoms may get more pronounced. While these symptoms can cause worry and fear in you, there is nothing to worry about. Some of these side-effects, and ways you can help your partner manage them, are as follows:

- **Morning sickness.** For some women, this can last all day. Morning sickness tends to peak around the second month of pregnancy, and it's thought that hormones play a role in this side effect, although physicians aren't entirely sure what triggers morning sickness (Holland, 2021). As the second trimester begins, the morning sickness should ease a little, eventually tapering off.

Here's what you can do: have a good supply of saltine crackers next to the bed, just in case your partner needs to eat a few before getting out of bed. These help ease the nausea of morning sickness. Make sure there is plenty of water in the home, and encourage your partner to drink some every morning. If you notice things seem too intense, call your partner's doctor with any questions or concerns for her. Don't forget to ask your partner how she is feeling; discussing the issue with her might help calm her, and you can decide together if a trip to the doctor's office is in order.

- **Motion sickness.** Some women have an especially hard time with driving, riding in a car or bus, and going on anything that moves. Sometimes, the nausea is so severe, they might have to pull over and vomit.

Here's what you can do: remain calm when these episodes of nausea happen. It's completely normal, even though it may be uncomfortable for you both. If you are driving, try to be gentle on turns, don't speed, and foster a calm environment with calming music. Your partner may be able to take motion sickness tablets to help; if so, consider storing a bottle of this medication in the glove box.

- **Minor bleeding and cramping.** This is also called spotting. Largely, this is due to the fertilized egg implanting on the uterus lining, and it can cause a level of bleeding similar to a light period. The blood can be pink, red, or brown and is usually never enough to need a menstrual product. Your partner may feel some pain but usually less than a menstrual cramp. This process can last anywhere from a few hours to three days (Holland, 2021).

Here's what you can do: stay calm and encourage your partner to take a break. Lying down and resting can improve this symptom. You'll also want to encourage your partner to avoid using any types of drugs, cigarettes, vape pens, or drinking alcohol during this time. She should also avoid tampons during this time as they may increase infection risks (Holland, 2021). Consider spending the day inside, resting in bed with your partner, and tending to her needs. If you can't be home with your partner, check in often. Remember that there is nothing wrong with seeking medical attention if you get uncomfortable with the amount of blood, your partner's discomfort, or for reassurance.

- **Odd cravings.** Everyone knows this one! Pickles and ice cream? Probably disgusting to everyone but your partner. However gross, it's totally expected and normal.

Here's what you can do: let her eat whatever she wants and walk away if your gag reflex starts acting up. She might laugh at you, though.

- **Frequent urination.** Pregnancy causes the body to pump more blood, thus increasing the kidneys' filtration process, leading to more urine in the bladder. Hormones also have a role in the function of the bladder (Holland, 2021).

Here's what you can do: be mindful of your partner's changes and be patient with how often she kicks you out of the bathroom. It can't really be helped, and remember that this won't last forever.

- **Extreme fatigue.** This fatigue is largely due to a hormone named progesterone rising in the body, which induces exhaustion. While this symptom can occur at any point during pregnancy, it's important to note that it can be difficult for a woman during the first few months as they may not be used to being so fatigued (Holland, 2021).

Here's what you can do: encourage an early bedtime, sleeping in, or napping during the day if possible. Also, consider lowering the thermostat to keep the home cooler, which can make your partner feel more energized and less incentivized to sleep as often. Sleeping too much may have an emotional impact where they are upset at how much work or life they are missing.

- **Tender breasts.** Tingles, aches, and growing breasts are a normal and common part of pregnancy. Typically, this happens in the second month of pregnancy and is the result of hormone levels changing rapidly in the body. As your partner's body adjusts to the changing hormone levels, this symptom will fade to a much more manageable degree. Later in pregnancy, your partner's nipples and areolas will change, as well, getting darker and larger (Holland 2021).

Here's what you can do: be particularly gentle with this area of your partner's body during intercourse. Normal affection you may have engaged in with this area during intercourse may cause her too much pain or discomfort. Ask your partner about the discomfort there, as needed. Also bear in mind that even a too-tight hug may cause pain and unease during this time, so it is best to be gentle and observe how your partner reacts to your touch.

- **Mood swings and irritability.** The culprit? You guessed it: hormones. Estrogen and progesterone levels go up, impacting moods and causing emotions to run high. This is incredibly common during pregnancy and can often cause irritability, anxiety, feelings of euphoria, or even depression in your partner.

Here's what you can do: be on the lookout for depressive moods and be especially attentive to your partner when these emotions are present. Your partner deserves to feel happy during this time, and that can be difficult when she is struggling with the hormonal changes in her body that cause mood swings. Talk to your partner about their emotions and their emotional state of mind. Gently ask them if they've felt depressed and if they'd like to seek out a mental health counselor. Sometimes, a therapist can be the best option for your partner's emotional health.

- **A change in temperature.** This is normal during pregnancy and is nothing to worry about.

Here's what you can do: bring your partner water and encourage her to use caution during exercise.

- **Higher blood pressure.** This can be scary for both yourself and your partner, but this symptom usually doesn't last very long in the pregnancy. During the early stages, blood vessels become dilated for higher blood flow and can cause dizziness (Holland, 2021).

Here's what you can do: follow up with your partner's primary care physician, first and foremost. You and your partner may want to start keeping a daily log of blood pressure measurements using an in-home blood pressure cuff you can purchase from the pharmacy. Show these numbers to your partner's primary care physician and help her doctor monitor any noticeable changes. Suppose anything is out of the ordinary or her doctor wishes to be extra-cautious. In that case, your partner's doctor may want to run some additional tests to monitor the electrical pulses from the heart. During any tests, keep calm and remind yourself that it's good to run tests during the early stages of pregnancy to ensure both mother and child are as healthy as possible.

- **Heartburn.** Hormone changes can cause the valve between the stomach and esophagus to loosen, leading to stomach acid leaking (Holland, 2021).

Here's what you can do: encourage your partner to eat frequent and small meals instead of larger ones. Ask her how bad the heartburn is and have a good supply of antacids, if needed.

- **Some acne.** As hormone levels in the body change at a rapid pace, acne pimples may crop up.

  Here's what you can do: truthfully, the best idea is just to ignore this one. It's entirely normal, and her skin will clear up as her body adjusts to hormone levels. If your partner is sensitive about it and wants a shoulder to cry on, you may want to reassure her that she's beautiful and that you love her.

- **Increased heart rate.** During weeks eight to ten, the heart may pump harder and faster, triggering palpitations and arrhythmias. These side effects are common in pregnancy and can be attributed to hormone changes (Holland, 2021). Studies reviewed in 2016 showed that blood flow tends to increase by anywhere between 30 and 50 percent during pregnancy, making the heart work harder. If your partner has a family history of heart conditions or an underlying heart condition, you will both want to speak to her primary care physician and obstetrician to address any concerns.

  Here's what you can do: encourage your partner to rest, seek medical attention as needed, and monitor any recent developments in palpitations and arrhythmias. You and your partner can speak to your partner's medical care team and plan to deal with any seemingly abnormal heart-related issues during pregnancy and beyond.

Cooperating & Sharing the Burden

As previously discussed, pregnancy symptoms are vast and usually attributed to hormone levels in the body changing at a rapid pace. However, testosterone levels in men decline during the early stages of their partner's pregnancy (Doheny, 2014). This decline is gradual, but no one yet knows why the hormonal change occurs in men. Researcher Robin Edelstein conducted a study on 29 expectant couples and found that hormone levels in women increased while testosterone and estradiol in men decreased (Doheny, 2014). Edelstein states that the decline in testosterone is not enough to classify the men in the study as having "low testosterone," but suggests that the reason for this decline could be that men with lower testosterone levels are less aggressive and thus better caregivers.

Overall, what this proves is that changes in pregnancy do not affect only women. Instead, it is a group effort between partners, and you should meet this burden with cooperation. This means both partners might find it difficult to manage the moods, but these changes can be handled through open and honest communication. The emotional support that you and your partner should exchange includes the following:

- Talking. A lot. Sharing what you need from each other is deeply important during this time. Clearly, you won't want to ask your partner to run marathons with you, but asking if you can attend visits and sonograms and be part of all major testing decisions is a great place to start. You may also want to discuss labor and what your role during that process should be. Some mothers may not be comfortable with their partners in the room while they give birth, so this topic is crucial.
- It's also important to share your emotions. "With all the attention on the mom and baby, you may feel ignored," an article from MottChildren.org states, "it's also common to feel nervous..." (n.d.). Discussing any feelings of neglect or negativity can help you both get on the same page. You and your partner may want to set aside an hour a day to simply discuss your emotions and feelings to keep you both in a mental state of peace.
- Ask questions at doctor's visits. By both engaging in the

process, you can increase your knowledge and your partner's knowledge about what is happening with your child and your partner. Sometimes, one of you may have a question that the other hadn't even thought to ask.

- Engage in conversations with other couples with children. Getting their expert advice and opinions can help you and your partner understand the road ahead for your family.

Keep in mind that you and your partner are the ultimate team and create the foundations for a family together. Talking to each other and discussing emotions together is of the utmost importance— especially as hormones change for both of you and you prepare for the next stage of your lives together.

Baby Development: Month Two

The second month of gestation is truly amazing for both parents to think about. During this time, your baby's face is developing, each ear beginning to fold at the side of their head, and their limbs begin to take shape. During this time, fingers, toes, and eyes also begin to form. "The neural tube (brain, spinal cord, and other neural tissue of the central nervous system) is well-formed. The digestive tract and sensory organs begin to develop," states WebMD's article entitled *The First Trimester: Your Baby's Growth and Development in Early Pregnancy* (n.d.). At this time, your child is now considered a fetus and weighs only about one-third ounce.

This is the perfect time to shop around for a gynecologist and obstetrician that both you and your partner are comfortable with. There are usually many options, and it's okay to go with the option that feels the best for you both—although your partner will get the ultimate choice as it is her body that will be examined.

When at the OB/GYN's office, you will likely hear your baby's heartbeat for the first time during the second month. Typically, this is a small speaker connected to a handle swiped over your partner's belly until the baby's heartbeat is located. This sound is a fast-paced swishing noise that you will likely remember for a lifetime.

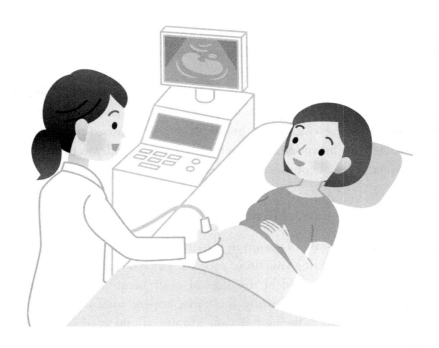

During this month, you may have your first ultrasound, which you'll want to embrace wholeheartedly. Not only is this test necessary, but for many parents, it can be life-altering. An ultrasound will rule out the possibility that the pregnancy is ectopic, first and foremost. An ectopic pregnancy is the result of a fertilized egg implanting somewhere other than the "main cavity" of the uterus ("Ectopic Pregnancy," n.d.). Often, the fertilized egg gets stuck in the fallopian tube, which carries a woman's eggs from the ovaries to the uterus every month. Ectopic pregnancies are nonviable, and if left untreated, mothers are at risk. An ultrasound will give you, your partner, and your partner's medical team the ability to verify that the pregnancy is not ectopic and that the baby is developing as needed.

This is the first time you'll get to see your child. Usually, pictures are printed out for you to take home, frame, and marvel at. Your partner will also be sent for blood tests to make sure that plasma protein A and HCG levels are in a normal range.

Tip #2: Get Car Maintenance & Home Maintenance Done Now

Babies require a lot of work and attention. When your new bundle of joy has arrived, you and your partner will be absolutely exhausted. That means you should take care of any major renovations right now instead of waiting for the pregnancy to progress or your child to arrive. In the later stages of pregnancy, you and your partner will likely be focused on getting the nursery in order and baby-proofing the home before your child begins crawling. This means that now is the perfect time to make sure the car has great tires, the oil is changed, the air conditioner in the house is working right, and the home's plumbing is working as it should be. Taking care of these things now will free up your time and energy to help take care of your partner, your baby, and yourself when the exhaustion hits. The last thing you'll want to do after a long workday is figuring out how to tear down your kitchen cabinets while your baby is trying to nap.

4

THE FIRST TRIMESTER - MONTH THREE

This is the last leg of the first part of your partner's pregnancy! You've made it through quite a bit already, and this month will mark a huge milestone in your new life with your partner. Give yourself some credit and cut yourself a lot of slack. The future may have some rough patches, but this is a time to celebrate.

In this chapter, we'll discuss one of the biggest things you'll need to tackle thus far: finances. Babies are notoriously expensive, and this means you'll have to engage in everyone's favorite activity. That's right: budgeting. This month, difficult pregnancy symptoms will begin to ease a little, and you'll have some breathing room to focus on building a better world for your baby. Let's get down to business.

Make Your Do's and Don'ts

Financially there's a lot to do before your baby arrives, and now is the best time to formulate a financial plan on how you're going to get everything that you and your partner need. The following Do's and Don'ts lists may not apply to you, but they may offer you some insight into what to think about, add, or subtract from the lists. For example, families living in colder climates may want to prioritize winter clothing for their babes, while families living in tropical climates may simply require light sweaters.

Take what you can from the lists, add your own items, and subtract what you don't need.

Do:

- *Think about the nursery and initial baby needs.* Initial needs would include a crib, changing table, a glider or rocking chair for your partner, a breast pump, clothing, and swaddling blankets. Diaper genies are also fantastic for your child's nursery, and some would argue they are completely necessary. By calculating the rough cost of these items, you can work toward saving up for these purchases.
- *Think about recurring baby needs.* Diapers, baby wipes, clothing, formula, and baby-friendly laundry detergent are all must-haves for a lot of families. Some partners seek to ease the cost of their baby's arrival by transitioning to cloth diapers or using soft cloths instead of wipes. It's time to consider all your options and decide where to best spend your money to optimize your child's arrival into your home. You may notice that clothing was listed both as an initial and recurring need for your baby; you'll be surprised by how quickly your baby will grow and how fast their clothing will not fit them anymore. For the first year, your child will likely grow out of their clothing every two or three months, and thus clothes shopping will likely happen between four and six times within the first year— just for your baby. Your partner will also need clothing as maternity clothing will no longer be necessary, and her previous clothing may not fit as well. Both situations should ideally be accounted for.
- *Think about healthcare and insurance needs for your baby and*

partner. Now is a perfect time to get familiar with your insurance information and employee benefits. We'll discuss this further later in this chapter.

Don't:

- *Wait until the last minute to get things done or make a financial plan for your family's needs.* Waiting until your baby has arrived will set you back with your needs. Having an appropriate budget in place can help with the challenges of caring for an infant.
- *Forgo a savings account during the pregnancy.* However compelling it may be to say, "I'll save up later" and spend a ton of money on a bunch of new baby stuff, it's important to wait and pace your spending. This pacing can help you and your partner build healthy spending habits and get things as you need them instead of filling your home with things you won't need for several months.
- *Forget your own needs.* Things like clothing, shoes, and groceries are still important, and you need them. Don't forget to take care of your own needs for the sake of spending money on your baby's furniture or diapers. It's okay to look for cost-effective options, sales, or coupons, but never skip out on your own needs.

Employee Benefits and Financial Planning for New Fathers

During this time, have a sit-down with an HR representative from your benefits department at work and discuss the coming changes in your dependents and household. The benefits department can help you examine your insurance coverage and discover how to include your child in your healthcare plan. Typically, healthcare plans can be modified when a life-changing event has occurred, which is what your child's birth would constitute as. As such, your child can be retroactively covered under certain insurances or added *in utero*. Discuss your options with HR and ask them to help guide you toward the best option for your family's needs.

Typically, employee benefits include healthcare, vision, dental, life insurance, and a 401(k) retirement account that often comes with employer matching. An employee will match the amount that an employee contributes to their retirement account. The advantage to a 401(k) plan is that this money is untaxed. Worker's compensation, flexible spending accounts (FSAs), and health savings accounts (HSAs) are also common employee benefits that can provide incredible value to a family welcoming a child (Griffin, 2017). An HSA, for example, is an untaxed account for medical treatment and prescriptions. This account can be incredibly useful for a family who has a more-than-typical amount of medical expenses, such as families with children who need inhalers or any other type of specialized treatment. Employers also usually offer paid vacation and time off, medical leave, paternity and maternity leave, and education assistance. Some of these benefits can make a world of difference as you transition into fatherhood. For example, paid time off will be invaluable for family trips, vacations, or watching your child in the school play!

Reviewing your employee benefits and understanding what costs your insurance plan covers for your child is only the first step in financial planning for your child's arrival. Several things can improve your understanding of life going forward and steps you can take to make the transition to your future life as smooth as possible:

- *Update your last will and testament.* While it's uncomfortable to think about—especially as you and your partner bring a new baby into the world—reviewing your will is an important part of being a parent. If anything were to happen to you, you'd want your partner and child to be cared for and happy. Writing your will can give you peace, knowing that your wishes will be granted and that your family will be financially stable. Other documents to think about updating include those involving your financial "accounts, including a health care directive, asset distribution and beneficiaries (including the percentage allocated to each beneficiary for every account), and power of attorney" (Abramson, 2019).
- *Invest in life insurance.* As previously mentioned, if something happens to you, you'd want your family to be taken care of. A life insurance policy can stabilize their lives and make the transition and grieving processes easier.
- *Create a rough household budget.* Life doesn't play by the rules, but guidebooks certainly help. By going through expenses and figuring out what you need and want, you and your partner can make a sensible financial.
- *Put more into an emergency fund.* Emergencies and children can go hand-in-hand. Having enough money for hospital trips, days off with a sick child, or getting laid off, can help you transition smoothly from one life event to the next.
- *Invest in childcare as early as possible.* Childcare, daycare, and babysitters are notoriously expensive. Because of this, getting a nine-month headstart can prove incredibly useful. You and your partner may want to shop around before settling on the closest or most convenient option. Many facilities offer tours of their establishment and may have discounted offers for the first few months.
- *Automate bill payments.* Some bills can be automatically deducted from a bank account when it is due. This is a

simple method to use, so you and your partner don't miss payments and get charged exuberant late fees or interest charges.

- *Consider how big a home you need without rushing to find an answer right away.* Some couples may want to purchase a larger home right away, but this may not be necessary. Children grow fast, but it can take them years to be comfortable in their own space. Some parents choose to co-sleep or move the crib into their bedroom for the first year of a baby's life. You and your partner have plenty of time to decide how much space you need and determine the amount of money you'd ideally like to spend on your housing.

Where's Your Savings Account At?

A savings account has never been more important—or beneficial—until this moment. Children are basically the manifestation of a wrench thrown into the plan that is life. They get sick sometimes and may need you or your partner to call out from work, which means missing a whole day's worth of pay. Having a cushioned savings account will assist with the pressure. Before your child arrives is the ideal time to build up that savings account as you have fewer expenses during this time. Ideally, you will want to have three to six months' worth of income saved into your account for emergencies or life changes.

A retirement fund is entirely different from a savings account. Retirement is for your future self at around age 65. At that time, you can merge the accounts, but you can use a savings account for surprises, life changes, or any other event that might set you off course.

Baby Development: Month Three

It's time to think about how your child is growing *in utero*. As the third month comes to a close, your baby is nearly completely formed—it's the size of a serving of shredded cheese (28 grams or one ounce, if you're wondering). At about only 3–4 inches long, your child now has arms, legs, hands, feet, toes, and fingers. It has started opening and closing its fists and mouth ("The First Trimester," n.d.). The teeth are now just starting to grow inside its skull; you may not have known this, but yes, babies are born with all their primary teeth already inside their skull, and as they grow, those teeth push down through the gums ("Teeth Development," n.d.). At this time, an ultrasound will still have difficulty determining the sex of your child, but their reproductive organs are developing. Also, "the circulatory and urinary systems are working, and the liver produces bile" ("The First Trimester," n.d.). As the third month comes to a close, the chances of a miscarriage drop dramatically, and the most critical functions of your baby's body are now developed.

Your partner will likely do some more blood tests and maybe have an ultrasound to ensure that everything is developing as it should. The appearance of twins or triplets will be much easier to tell during this time.

Tip #3: Gender Disappointment is Normal
While you'll absolutely want to keep the disappointment to yourself, it's normal to feel that way. You won't be finding out the sex of your child for another few weeks, but it's important to get used to the idea that the visions you may have had about your child may not come true. Get used to the idea of either gender popping up on that ultrasound early so that you can maintain a level of joy and happiness when you both discover what you'll be having.

5

THE SECOND TRIMESTER - MONTH FOUR

You've officially made it out of the first trimester! Only two more to go and the worst of those pregnancy symptoms should be coming to a close. This will leave plenty of time for more preparation and excitement. Many couples decide that the beginning of the fourth month is the best time to announce their pregnancy and interact with other pregnant couples. In this chapter, we will discover what you and your partner can do to help the fourth month go smoothly, as well as discuss how your baby is developing in the womb.

Announcing Your Partner's Pregnancy

The risk of miscarrying has dramatically decreased, so couples often decide to announce their pregnancy as the fourth month opens. Discussing the pregnancy with family members and close friends can be a time of pure bliss, filled with well-wishes and excitement all around. Be careful whom you tell first, as they will be the foundation of your support system for the rest of the announcements. Some people choose to call their parents first, while others seek out best friends more around their own age. However, you and your partner can wait longer if you're feeling uncomfortable, rushed, or you need more time to get used to the idea of pregnancy and being open about the pregnancy.

This is also the best time to tell your employer so that you have plenty of time to get your benefits in order and work with your employer on how to get your paternity leave situated.

There are no hard and fast rules when it comes to announcing the presence of your new bundle of joy. How you and your partner make those announcements is entirely up to you. Here are some of the most common options that are both efficient and fun:

- Announcement cards. Using these and mailing them out can make a fun and cute souvenir the whole family can keep. This can also make the announcing process easier, as everyone will know without having to call everyone.
- A social media post. Making an entry onto one of your social media accounts can be a great way to get the

message out without a big fuss. Be advised, however, that this method may draw in a lot of unsolicited advice, personal horror stories from other parents, or unwanted attention. As long as your friend and family group is supportive, a social media post can be ideal.

- Have a party. For the extroverts, a party is a must to make this announcement. Some couples may want to see and hear the shock on all their close relatives as they announce that they're going to be parents.
- Personal phone calls. Making personalized phone calls can be exhausting, and likely, by the time you get to the end of the list, the person you're calling might already know the news from another friend or relative. Regardless, this method has a personal component that might touch the caller.
- A video or photo upload. One of the best ways might be a video or photo, announcing the pregnancy to friends and family and sharing the excitement. The visual component differs from a simple social media post in that it is more personal. Tag your friends and family to make an even greater impact.

The bottom line to remember is that it doesn't matter which method you choose, just that your announcement is met with support and love from your closest friends and family.

Interacting With Other Soon-To-Be Parents

Having others to talk to about the progression of your partner's pregnancy is ideal, but having another soon-to-be dad to discuss things with can make a world of difference in your understanding of life. As you embark on the journey toward fatherhood, you may find that your friends ask you to hang out less or simply don't understand your plights when you express them. In these cases, you may want to interact with others who are in the same boat as you. This isn't to say you should drop all of your before-pregnancy friends. In fact, you shouldn't; strengthening the bonds you have with your current friends can help them understand your experiences while helping you maintain emotional stability as your life changes.

However, new friends who understand your situation more can help you have someone to rant to and exchange advice and life experience with. You and your partner may want to grab a coffee (or non-caffeinated tea for your partner) with another couple from a prenatal class, Facebook groups for soon-to-be parents, or couples that your partner may have met while shopping for baby clothes. You can also interact with these to-be dads online and talk there if that makes you more comfortable. You can try forum sites like Reddit.com, which has many boards for dads and fatherhood-related information.

Baby Development: Month Four

This month, your baby's fingers, toes, eyelids, eyebrows, eyelashes, nails, and hair are all forming. Bones become much sturdier, as do their teeth. Your child is now sucking their thumb, yawning, and stretching ("Fetal Development," 2020). You may be able to see them doing this during the ultrasound if you and your partner are particularly lucky. During this time, the reproductive organs are viewable and identifiable, which means that this is the big moment where you and your partner can find out whether your child will be assigned male or female upon birth. Your child is still incredibly tiny: about six inches long and only weighing four ounces. There's much more growth to go, but your child's major functions are developed and in working order.

During this month, your partner may require more blood tests. However, things should be smooth sailing within the fourth month.

Tip #4: Your Partner May Have an Increased Libido

As your partner enters the fourth month of pregnancy, some symptoms may begin to subside and be replaced with an increased sex drive. Her breasts may be much less tender and sore than before and may enlarge in size as her body prepares for the arrival of your child. After the baby is born, there may be a time when you and your partner cannot engage in intercourse because of exhaustion, doctors' orders, or anxiety about her body (from either of you). During this time, enjoy the sexual intimacy that you and your partner can share. Now is the time to connect emotionally, mentally, and sexually with your partner. Enjoy it, and don't worry about hurting the baby because you won't (unless her doctor has said otherwise).

6

THE SECOND TRIMESTER - MONTH FIVE

The fifth month marks the halfway point between the beginning of the pregnancy and the end (a pregnancy usually lasts 40 weeks, meaning it's closer to ten months than the common belief of nine). The most critical time in your baby's development is over, and your child is growing into a healthy and strong baby who will arrive in a few short months. Now is the time to start thinking about your child and what their life will look like—beginning with gender and names.

Finding Out the Gender

Most often, couples decide to find out what gender their baby is and base a lot of their future decision-making on this information. While it can be incredibly helpful to know this information, some couples don't want to know their baby's gender before they're born. The reasons you might want to wait include these serious concerns:

- *Stereotypes and gender bias issues.* Excited grandparents and family members might be pressuring you for this information simply because they want to know what color toys to buy or if they should shop for pink dresses. However, if you and your partner don't want to be influenced by knowing the gender of your baby, you can wait for the birth to find out.

- *You can reuse the gender-neutral baby clothes for baby #2!* If you and your partner want to have a second child, the barrage of gender-neutral clothing given to you at the baby shower can be incredibly beneficial.
- *The desire for mystery.* Some parents note that the mystery of not knowing the gender of their baby makes the rest of the pregnancy that much more fun. Some parents feel that, by waiting, the birth of their child is even more magical than knowing beforehand.
- *Incentivize labor!* As mentioned in the last bullet point, the mystery can be exciting, but the birth can be magical. Not knowing whether you're going to have a son or a daughter can make the big reveal even more spectacular.
- *Sometimes, the ultrasound is wrong.* With any test, there is room for error, and "while the number of errors seems to have dropped in recent years, it is still possible" (Weiss, 2021). Mothers and fathers who were particularly wishful for a certain gender might feel disappointed when their baby's gender differs from what they expected. The disappointment can lead to depression and may make one or both partners less prepared or happy for the birth of their child. In their article for Very Well Family, Weiss calls this a "mental miscarriage" (2021). If you and your partner choose not to find out the sex of your child, this removes any disappointment from your mind. Instead, you both can continue to romanticize walks down the street with either your son or your daughter.
- *Medically speaking, ultrasounds can be unnecessary.* Sometimes, an insurance provider may not cover an ultrasound unless it is medically necessary, and this

ultrasound may not be necessary for your partner's pregnancy. As such, some partners may not actually be able to find out their baby's gender beforehand.

- *The baby shower gifts are more useful.* With baby clothes mostly off the table (as the gender of the baby isn't known), you and your partner can expect to get things you might actually need more than dozens of onesies and shirts that your bundle of joy will grow out of in three months. Say hello to bottle warmers, diapers, diaper genies, and baby carriers—actual necessities.
- *You won't be asked so much about your names list.* Most people only ask about names after you've learned the gender of your baby. If you don't know the gender, you may not be asked so much about what names you're thinking about and what your partner wants. You have a hundred other things to do with your time than have the same conversation several times a day.

However, there are many benefits of knowing your baby's gender beforehand, mostly for couples who want to buy clothing and toys according to gender. There's also the extra preparation time that knowing your baby's gender provides. You and your partner can seek out detailed information and tips about changing diapers for baby boys or how to handle a diaper rash for a baby girl. This information can help if gender matters.

There are no rules for knowing your child's gender, and it's up to what you and your partner believe is the best course of action for your family.

Baby Names: How Do You Know What One Is the Right One?

Picking out the right name, or names if you want a middle name, can be difficult and scary. How do you pick a name that fits your child, that you won't hate in a decade, or one that won't become universally hated by society later down the line? It's not an easy task, but that is precisely the reason to start trying names out now, at the halfway point during pregnancy. You and your partner may have discussed a few names already, so now it's time to try them out and see which combination of names feels the correct fit for you.

Consider grabbing one of your child's sonogram pictures to look at while you play with the names. Try also imagining scenarios you think will happen in your future: playing catch, going roller skating, or bowling with your child. Imagine yourself saying, "great job..." What name comes to mind during those thoughts of the future?

You'll also want to discuss middle names with your partner and how all your child's names would go together. You certainly wouldn't want your child to have an easy-to-pick-on name. Try your hand at rhyming names with words as well; you may want to consider if "mouthwash Josh" is something you think your child can be teased over as they grow up. This means looking at initials as well. You want to make sure that your child's initials don't spell an obscenity, expletive, or any other inappropriate acronym. Children, as they grow, can bully other kids for basically any reason under the sun; you just don't want to give them any ideas or reasons to bully *your* child. Consider asking a child in your family what they think of certain names. They'll be brutally honest about it with zero care for your feelings at all, which is what you'll need.

Tread carefully when it comes to naming your child after any type of popular culture or celebrity trends. Naming your child after your favorite singer or character from a show may have negative repercussions later, especially if that celebrity does something unspeakable or the character becomes evil. You may want to look up lists of the most popular names and look through them to see if you and your partner like any of them. There's nothing wrong with picking a popular name!

Alternatively, you can also choose a specifically unpopular name from a different era in time, something from mythology, or a name from classic literature. The most important thing is that you and your partner love your child's name.

Baby Development: Month Five

As your partner carries your child into month five of pregnancy, your baby's hair begins forming all over their body, including the head, shoulder, back, and face. Your baby is also developing a coating that protects them from exposure to the amniotic fluid inside the womb ("The Second Trimester," n.d.). They will discard this before birth. As your baby begins developing and exercising their muscles, your partner may begin to feel the baby kicking inside them—a small, butterfly-like feeling called quickening. As the fifth month wraps up, your child is around ten inches long and can weigh anywhere between half a pound to a full pound.

During the fifth month, an obstetrician will perform a check-up on your partner. The obstetrician will check her for abnormal swelling, blood pressure range, the baby's heartbeat, the baby's growth, and take a urine sample to check sugar and protein levels (Weiss, 2021).

Tip #5: Sing to Your Baby *In Utero*

At this time, your baby can hear their mother's heartbeat, voices, and loud noises. Music and reading can be an incredible step in your baby's brain development. As the fifth month begins, you may want to begin singing to your child. While the voices may be harder for them to hear at this time, it can still be a great bonding experience for you and your baby. If you cuddle up close to your partner's belly and speak, sing, or read to your child, they can get accustomed to your voice before they arrive and thus feel more comforted by you when they meet you for the first time. During pregnancy, it can be hard for you to bond with your baby while in the womb, but singing to your baby and introducing them to your voice can have a huge payoff later.

7

THE SECOND TRIMESTER - MONTH SIX

Here you are: the last month of the second trimester. In this month, your partner's belly will continue to grow, and you may start to wonder how her body is even fitting a tiny human being in there. Thus far, you've likely been doing a lot of planning, preparing, and list-making. You may have started making purchases, storing away money, and discussing your financial status with an advisor. You may have even already discussed the details of your child's arrival date and benefits information with your HR department to get an idea on how to acquire paternity leave so you can be home to bond with your baby and partner when the time comes.

All of these steps are integral to your development as a father. You're making sure that your family is being taken care of and that your child has a smooth transition into the world.

In month six, it's time to take a well-deserved break and introduce some self-care and fun into your life. Month six is the perfect time for this. In the third trimester, your partner will likely be too tired for much of the fun stuff you both used to do, too exhausted to make food and have a more difficult time moving around. Enjoy this month of peace and comfort while you can. Trimester three is all about her and her comfort, so use month six as an opportunity to learn about self-care and how you can foster habits to take you through stressful situations.

Self-Care For Fathers

You may have heard the word *"self-care"* thrown around a lot lately. In the modern age, mental health and well-being are at the forefront of the world's mind—as they should be. After all, if you can't take care of yourself, how are you supposed to take care of your tiny human?

Self-care is "simply the act of taking time to focus on yourself" (Probasco, 2021). This can be a specific allotment of time each day or week that you set aside to focus solely on your needs and desires. There are no rules for self-care except that you enjoy yourself and that the act you are taking benefits your health, state of mind, or well-being. For some, self-care is making a full, nutritious meal that is enjoyable to make. For others, this might be tending to a garden, going for an extra gym session, or breaking out the miter saw for a woodworking project.

Self-care typically comes in five areas, and they all need to be adequately fostered to make a happy and healthy individual:

1. Physical. Physical self-care is anything that pertains to your physical body. This means going to a doctor, dentist, or nutritionist. It could also mean eating healthy, getting adequate exercise, and taking care of any sudden or persistent physical issues. For example, you wouldn't slap some duct tape on a broken leg and call it a day, right? No, you'd hop on over to the emergency room and have it cast and follow the proper medical advice on how to make sure it heals properly. Use this level of urgency to care for all aspects of your physical body. That means actively listening to your body's signals and taking care of them immediately. If your tooth has been hurting for a month, it's time to see a dentist; if your chest has been giving you pain, it's time to see a doctor. Your physical health is not a joke, a low priority, or a minor concern. It is of the utmost importance.

2. *Emotional.* This can be difficult for men who have been repeatedly told that emotions are not masculine or that dealing with emotions somehow makes them weak. Those ideas are simply not true. Unresolved trauma or emotional damage from early childhood can manifest in unexpected ways, such as deep insecurities, imposter syndrome, or angry outbursts. Unresolved emotional hurt from childhood issues can lead to chronic illness, health consequences like high blood pressure and cardiovascular disease, and difficulty "expressing anger in productive ways" (Raypole, 2020). There is no shame in journaling feelings, seeking affection and reassurance from your partner, and getting guided help from a licensed therapist.

3. *Intellectual.* This type of self-care is focused on intelligence and learning. This type of self-care includes picking up a new hobby, learning how to cook, or touring a cultural site. Anything that gives you information or helps you learn something new and applicable to your life can foster a feeling of excitement and zest for life. If you find yourself feeling stagnant and looking for something more, this can likely be the culprit of the empty feeling. Try doing or learning something new to assuage feelings of monotony.

4. *Spiritual.* This type of self-care does not inherently mean *"religious,"* but it can be for those who subscribe to religious beliefs. This type of self-care is anything that helps you connect with a higher power or a deeper understanding of the world around you. Some people may use this time to engage in meditation, yoga, running, or watching the sunset. Anything that helps you feel more connected to a spiritual or greater good will help improve your spiritual self-care.

5. *Professional.* No one wants to be swamped in work, but some people may want a career they are intensely proud of. If you strive to have a blooming career, it may be understandable for you to want a promotion and work long hours. This, however, can be tricky when you have a family to think about and spend time with. Discuss your career goals and desires with your partner and perhaps work out a plan for overtime hours that can help you achieve your goals while also being a present and loving part of your family dynamic.

By engaging in all five areas of your self-care once a week, you'll build habits that can help you get through the rest of your partner's pregnancy without succumbing to stress. These habits can also take you through the first, perhaps difficult, years of your child's life. Don't forget that fathers need self-care, too!

Sex & Pregnancy: What You Need to Know

Month six is the very tail end of the second trimester, which means much of the sexual fun may be coming to an end soon. And, when it ends, it may be gone for a while. Between your partner's pregnancy discomfort in the third trimester, birth, and recovery from birth, you and she may not have sex for a while. This is an unfortunate reality, but it will pass.

For now, you may have a few questions about sex during pregnancy, such as:

- Is it safe to have sex during pregnancy?
- Yes! Your child is protected by amniotic fluid inside the uterus and the muscles of the uterus. Sexual conduct won't impact the baby, assuming that there are no complications with the pregnancy.
- Can sex cause a miscarriage?
- No. Sex will not induce a miscarriage.

- What are the best positions for sex during pregnancy?
- There are no limitations for positions during pregnancy as long as you and your partner are comfortable. You may need to experiment to figure out what makes you both the most comfortable.
- Should we use condoms?
- Couples in long-term, monogamous relationships will not need condoms. However, still use condoms if you and your partner have slept with other people.
- When should sex be avoided during pregnancy?
- Late in the pregnancy, "breast stimulation, female orgasms, and certain hormones in semen called prostaglandins can cause uterine contractions" ("Sex During Pregnancy," 2020). Your partner's doctor might recommend avoiding sex in these situations:
- Unexplained vaginal bleeding.
- Leaking amniotic fluid.
- Cervical incompetence (where the cervix begins to open before it's time for labor).
- Placenta previa (where the placenta partially or entirely covers the cervical opening).
- History of premature birth.

If you and your partner are comfortable and the pregnancy is going without complications, feel free to engage in sexual intercourse without concern.

Baby Development: Month Six

As the sixth month of pregnancy comes to a close, your baby has grown two more inches and is now 12 inches long and weighs nearly two pounds. Try holding two pounds of fruit in your hands and seeing how it feels. That's how big your baby is.

Your child also has a reddish skin tone at this time, with wrinkles and visible veins through their "translucent skin" ("The Second Trimester," n.d.). Your child's fingerprints are also developing and visible, as well as their toeprints. At this time, their eyes can open, and they can blink. As the baby's hearing improves, they may respond to loud noises and movements. They can also hiccup at this point, and you may see them jerk in the womb as this happens ("The Second Trimester," n.d.).

This pregnancy obstetrician appointment will be very similar to the last. There will be a urine sample, measurements taken, and checks for any abnormal swelling or blood pressure ratings. You and your partner will also hear your child's heartbeat and ask any questions you may have.

 Tip #6: Discuss the Feeding Plan With Your Partner!

Now is the perfect time for you and your partner to discuss what you both think is the best form of nutrition for your baby. Many women choose to breastfeed, but many also decide that they've had enough of sharing their body and would rather bottle-feed their baby. There is no wrong choice, and both options are entirely valid. In the case of a breastfed baby, you may not be able to help as much as you'd like when the time comes. However, you and your partner can discuss making a plan in which she can pump some extra breastmilk for your child and store it in the fridge for you to warm up on nights when it's your turn to feed the baby.

If you and your partner decide that bottle-feeding or using both methods work well for your baby and your family, you can help out with feeding times as much as necessary. You may want to schedule who gets what nights so that you both get some rest and some bonding time with the baby.

8

THE THIRD TRIMESTER - MONTH SEVEN

With the second trimester at a close, you and your partner are entering the last third of the pregnancy journey. Things from here to the birth of your child may feel like a mixture of challenging and exciting. It may be difficult to wait, and you both may start to feel anxious about holding your baby, but the birth will be worth the wait. During the seventh month, you and your partner will decide what to pack for the hospital stay and learn about possible complications.

Time To Pack!

When it comes time to head to the hospital, there are about a hundred things that you'll think to bring, and you might still miss something. You might be so preoccupied with packing things for your partner or your baby that you might forget about your own needs. Make sure this doesn't happen to you—you'll thank yourself later. The best time to start packing your bag is right now, at the beginning of the third trimester. As the trimester continues, you'll think of other things to stick in your bag for the big day. Don't be surprised when you miss something, however. Babies run on their own schedule, and you may not have finished grabbing every little thing before your partner announces that her water has broken or that she is having contractions. There are three bags to worry about: one for your baby, one for your partner, and one for you. Your partner will likely take care of her bag, and you'll both work together to pack the diaper bag for your baby.

Here's a list of everything you'll need for your baby, though most of it will remain untouched, as the hospital will provide diapers, wipes, formula, and bottles for feeding:

- Extra diapers. You never know if your baby will have a very messy, blown-out diaper on the way home.
- A pack of sensitive wipes. The sensitive kind is best for newborns, as you aren't sure if your baby will have a bad reaction to the standard kind. The best time for experimentation will be later down the line.
- Extra clothes. For babies, three to four changes of clothes are ideal for keeping in the diaper bag and two sweaters during the cooler seasons.
- Three or four ziplock bags. You will use these to store dirty clothes, dirty bibs, used diapers so the smell doesn't permeate, and any other used or dirty messes.
- Pacifiers in a case or in a ziplock bag. A pacifier can be a great tool to assist with fussy babies and help them sleep easier and more soundly.
- Your baby's car seat! This is a must-have, of course. You won't be taking that baby anywhere without it.

You and your partner can discuss formula and bottle needs, but your diaper bag for the hospital will probably not need formula and bottles since your return trip will likely be without stops. Make sure, however, that you have formula stocked up at home to get you and your partner through the first week without needing to head to the store for resupply.

Your bag will likely be much larger and more detailed than your baby's bag. You'll need quite a few items:

- Ideally, two changes of clothes. Comfortable clothing will work best, which means sweatpants, sweaters, and pajamas.
- The most comfortable shoes you own.
- A pillow and blanket from home. The hospital will probably offer you a set, but they won't be particularly comfortable. Having your own set will make falling asleep easier—although you may not get a lot of it with a newborn in the room. You aren't likely to care about sleep that first night, however.
- Your basic needs: toothbrush, toothpaste, deodorant, shampoo, conditioner. The hospital might provide some small bottles of these and tiny brushes, but nothing compares to your own stuff.
- If you wear glasses or contacts, you'll need the essentials for those, as well. This includes contact solutions, glasses cases, and whatever else you may require.
- Snacks will be incredibly helpful if the birth lasts a long time or when the dust settles after your child is born. Think something prepackaged and easy to eat: trail mix or dried fruit.
- A reusable water bottle will be necessary. Many hospitals have recharge stations complete with vending machines, ice machines, water dispensers, and coffee makers. A reusable water bottle means you can fill up and spend the rest of your time with your partner and baby.

- Change for vending machines. Healthy snacks can get boring, so it's time to fill up on those terribly delicious snacks.
- Your camera and charger. You can have your own photoshoot in the hospital room, take pictures of your partner and baby, and remember the birth of your child for the rest of your life.
- A cell phone charger. Your cell phone will be much easier to remember, but you can easily forget your charger, and you'll probably need it.
- A Bluetooth speaker. Many parents like to play music during the birth of their child or use the speaker to play calming and upbeat music to help keep them relaxed.
- A written birth plan. This is what you want the birth of your child to be like. This includes if you want the room to be silent so you can hear your child's first breath or if there are any other specific requests you'd like to make.
- Any insurance information you may have.
- A "push present." This is a gift that you'll give your partner after the baby is born to show your appreciation for them and their hard work for your family.

Your things are packed but don't forget to toss your wallet and payment cards into your bag before you go. You'll likely need to grab some food the morning following your child's birth, and you don't want to run back home for your wallet. Consider everything that you and your family will need for a two-day trip and pack anything that comes to mind. It's much better to over than under pack.

What Complications Could Happen Now?

There's a lot that could happen at this point in your partner's pregnancy. Some of the most common complications include

- Premature birth. This is a birth that occurs "more than three weeks before the baby's estimated due date" ("Premature Birth," n.d.). The health impact of premature babies can vary, but typically those who are premature may be much smaller than usual, have sharper features, have fine hair covering their body, and have a lower body temperature than normal.
- Multiples not noticed on ultrasounds. Sometimes, the ultrasound may not capture the second baby at all due to the positioning of the first baby.
- Breech position. While most babies will get into position as the time nears for birth, some babies don't get the memo. The breech position is when the feet come out first, as opposed to the head. Many physicians will recommend a cesarean delivery, in this case, as it can be safer for both baby and mom.
- Placenta previa. This complication happens when the placenta is covering the cervix. Doctors usually recommend a cesarean delivery when this happens.

When the doctors discover a complication with your child's birth, the best possible thing you can do is to first remain calm. Your main priority should be making your partner feel comfortable because she's the one who has to give birth to the baby, either by vaginal delivery or cesarean section. For your partner, the world may be crumbling. You must remain a pillar for her.

Take deep breaths, try to slow your heart rate, and accept the reality of the situation without giving in to fear. Then, ask as many questions as you need to. Do not be afraid to ask questions. Make sure that you understand the full extent of the situation. The more questions you ask, the better. The lines of communication between you, your partner, and the team of physicians taking care of your partner and baby should be open and clear. Here are some good questions to ask:

- What happens next?
- What can we do?
- What are our options?
- What is the best course of action?
- How is the health of the baby?

With patience, communication, and calmness, you and your partner will get through this tumultuous time.

Baby Development: Month Seven

Your baby is growing like a stubborn little weed! As the seventh month of pregnancy continues, your baby is gaining fat deposits all over their body. They are likely about 14 inches long and weigh anywhere between two and four pounds! Your child's hearing is now fully developed, and they can hear things outside the womb, including loud, sharp, or frightening sounds ("Your Baby's Growth," n.d.). This means your baby will start to recognize the voices of the people they hear the most. Take time to talk to your baby in the womb so that they can recognize who "dad" is.

During this month, your partner will have her vitals checked at the doctor's office, provide a urine sample to screen for sugar, infections, and protein levels. The doctor will also evaluate the baby's heartbeat using a Doppler device. Fundal height—the size of your partner's stomach between her pelvic bone and the top of her uterus—will also be measured to make sure that the baby is growing in a good range (Ayuda, 2021).

 Tip #7: Start Buying Nursery Items This Month To Build Next Month

It can take months to put together a nursery in a way that satisfies you and your partner. You may think you want the room set up a certain way but then change your mind. This process will take time and energy. Start buying all of the items you need in the seventh month so that months eight and nine consist of setting it up for your baby's arrival.

9

THE THIRD TRIMESTER - MONTH EIGHT

By the eighth month, you and your partner are halfway through the third trimester and getting closer and closer to the end. In the eighth month, you'll set up the nursery, start prenatal classes, and go to a few more prenatal appointments.

Setting Up The Nursery

Setting up the nursery is all about what you and your partner prefer. There are, however, some tips you may want to consider. Here are some possible do's and don'ts:

Do:

- Buy a glider. Trust me. You're going to need it. Middle-of-the-night feedings will be way more comfortable in a glider than anything else. "Make sure it's comfy because you'll be spending a ton of time in it," says blogger Angela Lanter in a 2018 post to her site. It's true: the glider is invaluable.

- Invest in a soft rug or carpet for the nursery floor. In just a few months, your baby will be rolling around the floor, and you don't want any scrapes or bruises from the hard floor.
- Browse cribs that grow with your child. Some cribs come with extra parts and will transform into toddler or twin-size beds so that your child will have a bed frame to use as they grow. A crib mattress can be switched out for a twin-size when your child is older enough.
- Get things organized. Clothing, diapers, wipes, and formula should all have a place so that late-night feedings or changings won't be too difficult or disruptive—especially in the first few months.
- Add your flair. If you're a good artist, painter, or carpenter, add something just from you to your baby's nursery. This can be a rocking chair, art on the wall, or a gift your child can use in their own nursery when they become a parent. These keepsakes will mean a lot to your child in the future.

Don't:

- Put the glider next to the door to the nursery. The last thing your partner needs is to be woken up after a sleepless night with the baby to your getting-ready-for-work routine or by the doorbell going off due to some solicitor.
- Put the crib next to or under the window. That's a hazard waiting to happen.
- Forget blackout shades. These can make sure that your baby stays asleep so that you and your partner can get some much-needed rest. This can be a lifesaver for the first three months of your baby's life, as they will likely be up at all hours of the day and night.
- Be too shy or afraid to return something. There's a reason why people include a gift receipt with their baby shower

gifts—because you might not need it. If you don't need it, return it and use that money for something more beneficial.

- Choose themes that your baby will grow out of in a few months. Spending tons of money on room decor that will be useless in a few months will likely frustrate you to no end. Instead, look to beds that grow with your baby and furniture that they'll be able to use down the line.

Prenatal Classes: Why They're Important

The benefits of prenatal classes are often understated. They may seem like a tedious part of the pregnancy journey, but they have two major benefits: information and socialization. Some of the parents in the prenatal classes may be going through it again for their second child, which means you can get personalized and first-hand information from them about what raising a baby is like. It also means making connections and friendships with other people at the same stage in your life. These benefits cannot be stressed enough, as the journey of fatherhood can get lonely at times. Having other fathers to go to for help, guidance, and support can help keep you on your feet and feeling motivated. Not only will you learn all the basics, like holding and feeding, but you'll get some connection and friendship.

However tempting, try not to make jokes during the prenatal class. It may be hard to keep all your funny puns inside, but your partner will appreciate you keeping the jokes inside until you've at least made it to the car. Simply try to listen to the instructor and take notes as necessary. Also, take cues from your partner. Whatever they think is especially important, write it down for later.

Baby Development: Month Eight

Your baby has grown at least four inches and now is about 18 inches long and weighs about five pounds. Their body continues to put on fat stores, and they may be a lot more active inside your partner's womb. Their brain, during this month, is developing at a rapid pace, and they can now see and hear ("Your Baby's Growth," n.d.). Their organs are now well-developed, aside from their lungs, which will develop to absolute maturity in the ninth month of pregnancy. Overall, they are doing great, reaching the final stage of their growth *in utero.*

During this month, your partner will be undergoing the same procedures as the last month's doctor's visit, except for a cervical exam. This exam will give the doctor an idea of any possible dilation and confirm that things are going smoothly.

Tip #8: Babies Can Cry In The Womb

Although they make no sound, babies often cry in the womb. They can also suck their thumbs or toes, drink amniotic fluid, and get uncomfortable. Don't worry, though. Your baby's cries are nothing to be alarmed about. In fact, they are likely just practicing how to cry outside the womb and "imitating the breathing pattern, facial expression, and mouth movements of a baby crying outside of the womb" (Frost, 2020). There is nothing to worry about, but it's great to know your baby is doing their part by practicing how to operate outside the womb.

10

THE THIRD TRIMESTER - MONTH NINE

You and your partner have walked through challenges to get to the end of the pregnancy journey. At the end of this month, you'll be holding your baby in your arms and marveling at how small they are. You and your partner will spend a lot of time together with your baby and discuss your new lives as a family. In the final month of pregnancy, you'll read more about labor, when it's time to go to the hospital, and the birth.

Heading To The Hospital

A lot of fathers may not realize how fast the labor process can go for some women. "Usually, labor ranges from 6 to 18 hours from the very early stage until birth" ("What is Precipitous Labor," n.d.). This means contractions can last several hours, slowly coming closer and closer together until your partner's body is ready to push your baby out of the womb.

Often, your partner will have a discharge of something called the mucus plug. This is a jelly-like material, usually pink and clear in color, that comes out in the final weeks of pregnancy. Some women lose this plug right before labor, but it's not unusual for women to lose this plug at any time within the last three weeks of pregnancy (Weiss, 2021). If your partner loses this plug at an appropriate time during her pregnancy, there is no reason to go to the hospital for this. However, this is a sign that labor is coming soon.

"As a general rule, you know you are ready to go to the hospital when your contractions are 4 minutes apart, lasting 1 minute, for at least 1 hour" (Weiss, 2021). This is called the 411 rule, which means that these contractions are likely not Braxton–Hicks contractions. Braxton–Hicks contractions are mild contractions that happen as the uterus is preparing for delivery by practicing what it needs to do. These contractions will likely be mild, felt mostly in the front of your partner's body, and last less than 30 seconds each. Generally, contractions are serious if your partner is in pain and cannot speak through the contraction.

Another thing to consider is whether or not your partner's water has broken. Usually, her water will break just a few hours before birth. However, every woman, pregnancy, and baby is different. Some women experience broken water just before birth, while others have to have their waters broken for them. However, it is important to keep in mind that "the risk of infection increases if [your partner does] not give birth within 24 hours" of her water breaking (Weiss, 2021).

If there are other concerns, such as bleeding, dizziness, headaches, or blurred vision, then you and your partner should go to the hospital immediately.

While having contractions, your partner should not take any pain medications at home. She should consult with a physician before taking any medications at all, as some medications are not safe during pregnancy. Ibuprofen, for example, can cause an increase in congenital deformities (Bell, 2020). Other medications that should be avoided during any stage in pregnancy include:

- "Ibuprofen (Advil)
- Aspirin
- Naproxen (Aleve)
- Diclofenac (Voltaren)
- Codeine
- Morphine
- Oxycodone" (Bell, 2020).

However, Tylenol, in small doses, is often regarded as safe for pregnant women. Urge your partner to consult with her doctor about any concerns she may have about medications.

Another major aspect of the trip to the hospital is sorting out transportation. Pregnant women, especially those in labor, should not drive a car. A good idea to assuage the concern about transportation is to take a few days off from work to be home before the due date arrives. Talk to your employer about leaving work when your partner thinks she's in labor and taking time off to help her get to the hospital. It can also be a good idea to reach out to a relative or friend who lives close by for help.

At The Hospital

Carefully consider who you want in the room or waiting room when your baby is being born. This conversation should be a priority between you and your partner. Your partner may want her mother in the room while you prefer this to be just between you two. Ultimately, the birth will be her struggle and challenge, and she will be in a lot of pain during the process. Concede to what your partner believes is best for her comfort and your baby.

When you arrive at the hospital, you may be frantic, but try to remain calm. If your partner cannot speak, tell the nurses and doctors what they need to know. However, if she can speak, let her take the reins. Simply, try to assist her in a way that enables her to be in control and make the calls she thinks are best for her and your baby.

Sometimes, your baby might be late. "Most babies arrive between the 38th and 42nd weeks of pregnancy. When babies haven't arrived by week 42, they're considered late...One in ten babies is born post-term" ("What To Do," n.d.). Depending on your partner's health and your baby's health, your partner's physician might decide to induce labor if your partner is over one week past due; however, some doctors like to wait a few extra days to give your baby time to go into labor on their own. Your partner's doctor might decide to conduct a non-stress test, ultrasound, or other measurements to ensure your baby is developing as needed and there are no under-lying issues.

Ready To Meet You: Your Baby's Birth

If everything goes according to plan, you'll be at the hospital with your partner, who will be pushing and screaming. Keep your cool about it. It may scare you to see your partner in pain and pushing that hard, but it's completely expected and normal. It's worth the reward of your child coming into the world. Try to support her as she pushes.

Finally, you'll hear your child cry and watch as the physicians check them out for any anomalies. Next, you may be able to cut the umbilical cord. Some physicians may not allow this if there is an immediate concern, but cutting-the-cord is common practice.

Typically, nurses will use a bulb syringe to clean out any fluid or mucus from your baby's nose and mouth. This syringe is not sharp, and it's typically made of silicon so won't hurt your baby. Then, your baby will lie on your partner's chest for comfort since they will know who their mother is by scent and the sound of her heartbeat. Nurses may encourage your partner to immediately start breast-feeding the baby as your baby may actively seek out the comfort of being fed.

You may feel excitement building in your chest and a yearning to hold your child. Your time will come after your partner has had the moment to bond with your baby. She did, after all, just go through a lot of pain and discomfort to bring them life. Allow her some time to hold the fruit of her labor. If your partner is comfortable with this, this is a good time to take some pictures or memorialize the moment on video.

When you do get the chance to hold your baby, take a moment to feel everything that comes to you. You may have a mixture of emotions—it's okay to feel them all. Try to revel in this moment.

The Pediatrician Visit

Shortly after your baby's birth, your hospital room may have a lot of visitors in the form of lactation consultants, gynecologists, and pediatricians. The pediatrician will have a look at your baby, check out their vital signs, and take a look at all their limbs. The pediatrician is there for any everyday issues—even after you go home. Your pediatrician will take care of any rashes, concerns about the umbilical cord piece attached to your baby's belly, or feeding worries. They will be an integral part of your child's growth and development throughout the years. They will see your child many times in the first year and once a year until your child is an adult.

Tip #9: Your Baby's First Poop Might Scare You

Your baby, as you may know, does not poop in the womb. Instead, a tar-like, black substance called meconium blocks their digestive system. This first bowel movement won't actually smell bad, and it's sterile. This is because the intestines haven't been "colonized with bacteria, [so] there's nothing to make [their] poop stinky" (Hill, 2012). Most of the time, this bowel movement is made several hours after delivery, but with difficult deliveries or distress, a baby might release it *in utero*. Meconium will continue to pass from their system for a day or two, but eventually, you'll start to see—and smell—normal bowel movements coming from your bundle of joy in no time. So, don't be scared by the black, tarry stuff! It's totally normal.

11

BEING PREPARED—THE FIRST MONTHS

Your partner's pregnancy is over, and you both are now preparing for your first few months home with your new child. This is an exciting time filled with love, adoration, and change. The transformation to yourself and your partner will be a beautiful thing as you both embrace parenthood and grow together. You and your partner will want to prepare the home for your baby's arrival, learn how to hold a baby properly, discover the best ways to change diapers, and consider browsing through baby support groups or Mommy & Me groups in your area. Interacting with other families with babies helps you and your partner get a handle on how to handle your own child. All of this means baby-proofing, watching endless tutorials online, and learning firsthand by making mistake after mistake. After all, this journey into parenthood will not be without struggle, mistakes, or challenge. However, working with your partner, loved ones, and close friends, you will be able to handle your baby's first few months like pros.

Home Sweet Home: Interacting With Your Baby

There may be nothing sweeter than walking into your home for the first time with your newborn. You might feel a mixture of emotions, though. New fathers are no strangers to nervousness and anxiety. You may actually feel terrified at the lack of control you feel since you can no longer relax on the couch without first caring for your baby.

However, coming home is a great time to start bonding with your baby. You may not have had a lot of time with your child in the hospital since your partner was likely doing a lot of the feeding and cuddling with your child. Now, it's your turn to think of ways to hold, love, and bond with them. Newborns, notoriously, don't do much. They mostly eat, sleep, and poop. Do not let that stop you from trying to form a bond. Back rubs and skin contact can be great for babies. In fact, an article from Sanford Health states the following benefits for a baby to have skin-to-skin contact:

- "Better able to absorb and digest nutrients
- Better body temperature maintenance
- Cries less often
- Demonstrate improved weight gain
- Experience more stable heartbeat and breathing
- Higher blood oxygen levels
- Long-term benefits, such as improved brain development and function as well as parental attachment
- More successful at breastfeeding immediately after birth
- Spend increased time in the very important deep sleep and quiet alert states
- Thermoregulation
- Stronger immune systems" (Seitz, 2017).

You may want to consider starting a baby/father routine in which you spend time with your child by employing skin-to-skin contact. You can also sing, talk, and go for walks with your child.

You may have done some baby-proofing and preparing for your baby, and now it's time to relax. So tuck your baby into their crib or bassinet and take a nap or watch television. Your main priority should be adjusting to life with your newborn baby and discovering their temperament and attitudes. Try not to be frustrated by the things you can't do anymore, and instead, treat this time as learning time. Spend time with your baby in the nursery and get to know their space and them.

You might be spending time with your baby to give your partner a break from breastfeeding, a well-needed nap from being up a lot of nights, or letting them have time to themselves. This means finding ways to interact with your baby, which will include a lot of playing. "Play is the chief way that infants learn how to move, communicate, socialize, and understand their surroundings. And during the first month of life, your baby will learn by interacting with you" ("Learning, Play, and Your Newborn," n.d.). The way your touch feels, the way your voice sounds, and the way your face looks will be some of the ways your baby's comfort needs are met. Eventually, they learn that these signals mean they are in good, safe hands. The way you interact with them should reflect this comfort in the way you play. You may want to move their legs and arms to music and have them "dance." You may also want to invest in rattles, textured toys, musical toys, and plastic crib mirrors. Babies will find joy in toys that have contrasting colors and those that make plenty of sounds. Consider playing with your baby using these toys by moving them, letting your baby "get them," or by pointing out different colors. "Strong contrasts (such as red, white, and black), curves, and symmetry stimulate an infant's developing vision. As vision improves and babies gain more control over their movements, they'll interact more and more with their environment" ("Learning, Play, and Your Newborn," n.d.).

Other ideas include swaying to gentle music with your baby, singing lullabies, making silly or goofy faces at your baby, or letting your baby have some tummy time when they can support their head and neck. Don't forget that talking to your baby and reading to them also stimulate their brain.

How To Hold & Rock Your Baby

It's entirely normal for you, as a new father, to have a healthy level of fear about how to hold your baby and how to rock them to sleep. It can be terrifying to hold this tiny infant in your arms. However, with time and practice, you'll get used to it. In the meantime, here is a small rundown of the most important things to remember when it comes to picking up, holding, or cradling your newborn.

- When you first pick up your newborn, remember to support their head with your palm and be extra careful of the soft spots at the top of their skull. These soft spots are called fontanels, and they "are spaces between the bones of the skull where bone formation isn't complete" ("Video: Baby's Soft Spots," 2020). These soft spots make it easier for your baby to come out of the birth canal.
- When picking up your child from the crib or bassinet, slide one hand under your infant's head and neck while using the other to support their bottom. When you are confident with your hold, you can scoop your baby up and bring your baby close to your chest.

- To cradle your baby after having scooped them up, rest your baby's head against your chest and slide your hand up from your child's bottom to brace their neck. From there, move your baby's head to the crook of your elbow and place your other hand under your baby's bottom. This cradle hold will have your baby completely supported in your arms.
- You will also need to know the shoulder hold when burping your baby. This means you'll rest your baby on your chest and shoulder while supporting their neck and head with your hand. Place your other hand under your infant's bottom to keep them supported. When burping, you'll want to be seated and leaning just a little backward so that your baby will be pressed against your chest while your hand that would have been supporting their neck can pat their back to help burps emerge.
- It is never safe to carry your baby with one hand while the other is holding something dangerous like a knife, a hot pan, or a hot drink. Always place your baby in the bassinet or crib before grabbing your drink or making food.
- A very popular way to help your infant fall asleep is to rock them gently. This is usually done by swaying at the hips

while your baby is in a cradle hold. You may also slowly
walk or pace. Some parents like to walk around the home
and introduce their baby to the environment as they fall
asleep to bond with their baby.

Holding your baby may scare you some of the time, and you may
feel terrified of dropping your newborn, but you likely won't. It's
simply a matter of getting used to their small body in your arms.

How To Change Your Baby

Diaper changes will start as anxiety-inducing moments of panic for
many fathers, mostly because you may be afraid to bend your
baby's legs or move them in certain ways. You'll ask yourself about a
hundred times if you're hurting them or if they should be bending
that way, but you must trust yourself. Your baby will fuss and cry if
they are uncomfortable. The steps to changing a diaper are not too
hard to follow:

1. Lay your baby on the changing table (or a flat surface if
   you aren't home).
2. Unbutton your baby's onesie or take their pants off.
3. Undo the little plastic, velcro tabs of their diaper.
4. Open your baby's diaper and assess the extent of the
   change needed. You may require one wipe, but more often
   than not, you'll need a bunch.
5. Wipe your baby's diaper area until it is clear and there is
   no pee or poop left on the body. Be careful to check their
   back. Sometimes, a large amount of poop can go up their
   back instead of staying in the diaper.
6. Apply baby powder to keep from chaffing.
7. When your baby is clean, lift their bottom half and slide a
   diaper under their body.

8. Pull the diaper between their legs and attach the small velcro tabs back in place.
9. Dress your baby in a new onesie and pants if the previous one got dirty, or reclasp the previous onesie or replace their pants if they're clean.

Look at that! You just changed a diaper all by yourself.

The Feeding and Sleeping Problem: Breast Versus Bottle

In a previous chapter, we discussed the need to talk with your partner about sleeping/feeding needs in the middle of the night. You and your partner should make a schedule that conforms with work and home needs. You should be getting up to change and feed the baby on specific nights while your partner should be doing it on the opposite nights. The sleeping/feeding struggle will only work out if both partners are working together to balance the need for sleep. One of the best investments that all fathers can make is in a bottle warmer for the middle of the night. These can be relatively inexpensive and be a huge lifesaver during middle-of-the-night feedings.

Parents who wish to breastfeed exclusively may want to invest in a quality breast pump so that your partner can pump extra breast milk for you to feed the baby during your nights on duty. This can not only give your partner a break, but it can also help you bond with your baby. You and your partner can discuss how much extra she will need to pump and store. You'll also need to make sure how to warm up a bottle of breastmilk. These steps include

1. Grab a clean bottle and the stored breastmilk from either the fridge or freezer.
2. If the breastmilk is frozen, run it under some cool water from the faucet until it has melted.
3. Place the breastmilk in a bottle and place the bottle in a

bottle warmer. If you do not have a bottle warmer, you can place the bottle in a bowl, mug, or small pot of hot tap water (that is not boiling) for 15 minutes.

4. Test the temperature of the bottled breastmilk against the inside of your wrist.

Alternatively, you may take out a pack of frozen breastmilk every day for the nighttime feedings and leave it in the refrigerator.

It's even simpler for parents who want to use formula or both breastmilk and formula. You can simply mix warm water with the formula powder or open a pre-mixed formula bottle and use these immediately.

Make sure that after every feeding, you burp your baby. Any trapped gas can make your baby vomit or feel colicky. This is done with the shoulder rest hold, as previously mentioned.

When Nights Are Too Long: How To Make Baby Sleep

Some babies can be colicky, which means they have some discomfort or pain due to gas buildup. Colicky babies are characterized by crying a lot and not being able to get good sleep. This means that you and your partner will likely not get the best sleep either. Colic aside, some babies are just very picky about how they sleep and where. Babies are hardwired to seek out the sources of their basic needs. In many cases, this means their mother's presence is their most comforting feeling. Not only does their mother offer them the protection they were familiar with *in utero*, but also food, emotional reassurance, and warmth.

However, your baby will often not be able to get that comfort from their mother, but instead from you, their father. Thankfully, there are several handy ways to get your baby to sleep without too much fuss or drama. These include

- Swaddling. One of the most acclaimed methods for getting a baby to sleep, swaddling takes away the option for an infant to do anything else with their arms and legs. Pair this with rocking in a glider or rocking chair to help ease them to sleep. You can see the steps to swaddle your baby safely here:
- Spread the blanket out as a diamond shape and fold the top corner down.
- Place your baby on the blanket with the folded edge running along the neckline.
- Wrap one side of the blanket across your baby's body with arms inside the blanket. Tuck that side gently under your baby's back.
- Wrap the other side of the blanket in the opposite direction, tucking your baby into the blanket.
- Fold the bottom up and tuck it into one of the folds. Keep in mind that as your baby grows, you may not be able to tuck the bottom flap in as easily. This means you may want to keep socks handy to keep their little feet warm or invest in larger swaddling blankets.

Alternatively, you can do step "d" last to create a different type of swaddle. Experiment with both types and see which your baby is more comfortable with. The point is simply to make your baby "feel snug, warm, and secure" ("How To Swaddle," n.d.).

- Rubbing or massages. Some babies really enjoy rubbing between the eyes as this can encourage them to close their eyes, and it also feels great for them. Gentle massages to their limbs can also make them sleepy. Try doing these for five minutes when you want them to settle down.
- Swaying and singing. These two activities are the cornerstones of raising babies. A soft singing voice mingled with swaying from either a glider or their parent standing up can make a baby feel drowsy and easily fall asleep.
- Breast or bottle feeding. Having a full belly can make babies sleep much easier. Just be sure to feed them enough to make them drowsy and stop before they fall asleep, or else it may be harder for you to lay them in their crib.
- Play quiet, ambient music, or white noise. Some babies need noise to be able to rest. Using a sound soother or an app can help your baby get drowsy and sleep easier.
- Use dim lighting. Employing dimmer lights in the area your baby sleeps in can help them get used to the day and night cycles of their world.

However, with any of these methods, it's important to place your baby in their crib or bassinet when they are "drowsy, but awake" (McTigue, 2020). This will help them understand that they must learn how to soothe themselves to sleep on their own. They might startle or become fussy when you've placed them into the crib, but placing a warm hand on their belly and shushing them can be enough to help them settle down at times. Sometimes, you may have to repeat the process of helping them get drowsy and then placing them in the crib if they get themselves too wound up. However, with patience, your baby will learn the signs for bedtime under dad's supervision.

Miscellaneous Debates & issues: What You Need To Know

Many new parents must contend with several debates. These are unmeasurable, and just when you think you've got one solved, another takes its place. The following list is just a few of the debates that you'll have within the first few months of your child's life:

- *When do we give up breastfeeding?* Breastfeeding is the most natural form of sustenance for your child, and many pediatricians will recommend breastfeeding exclusively for at least six months and introducing other age-appropriate foods alongside breastmilk for one-year-olds or older ("What Are The Benefits," 2021). Breastfeeding has many benefits for both baby and mother. Breastfeeding lowers your child's risk of asthma, obesity, diabetes, and respiratory disease. Your partner can benefit from breastfeeding by having lower risks for breast cancer, ovarian cancer, diabetes, and high blood pressure. That being said, some women decide to breastfeed their children for up to two years. However, there is no shame in choosing formula if breastfeeding is too difficult for your partner or has adverse effects. Some women simply don't want to breastfeed, and there's nothing wrong with supporting your partner's choice for either option.
- *Newborns and pets.* It is entirely normal to have some anxiety about introducing your brand-new baby to your potentially rowdy and excitable animals. In fact, life with your pets will change when you introduce a baby into the home. "A study of nearly 600 dog and cat owners, which

was presented at the 2010 meeting of the American Sociological Association, confirms what most people believe to be true: Pet owners who have children spend less time with their pets" (Fields, n.d.). While this may be disappointing, it's a necessary facet to having children and pets. Instead of focusing on the lost time you'll have with your pet, you may wish to foster a loving and heartfelt connection between your child and your pet so that your child can share the same relationship you and your pet share.

- That being said, you should prepare your pets to accept your child's presence in the home. Try exposing them to the lotions you plan to use for your child and play child noises from online videos to help them become familiar with the sound of a baby crying or laughing. Sudden changes can be stressful for pets, so let them tour the nursery and get used to the new arrangement of the furniture.

- *Let them cry it out.* When a baby cries a lot, some old advice might be to let the baby "cry it out" and that it's good for their lungs to cry. Often, letting your child cry at night is considered the same as sleep training, but many sleep training methods don't involve ignoring your child's pleas for love, attention, and warmth. With sleep training, there is a certain amount of time that you and your partner will stay away to help your child understand that you *will* come back for them, although this amount of time will vary for each family. With the cry-it-out method, you simply don't come back, and your child may be scared that you will never come back. It's also unnecessary for sleep training to involve a lot of crying, fuss, and demands. Many approaches use gentler methods. It's all about finding the right sleep training method that works for your family.

Also, keep in mind that sleep training is an ongoing process requiring patience, time, and energy. You cannot expect to be done with sleep training after one bout of it. Sometimes, your child may relapse and need to be retrained. This is not abnormal and should be expected.

Sleep training is a great way to help your child foster their own independence in the long run. When your child is in control of their own sleep and understands how to self-soothe enough to fall asleep on their own, your life will be easier, your sleep will improve, and your child's confidence will increase.

- *Entertainment for newborns.* As mentioned previously, newborns live rather sedentary lifestyles until they're old enough for tummy time. Before tummy time (which should be around four months, when they can hold up their own head), they will likely enjoy simply looking around, playing with small rattle or teethers, and watching their parents. Small, unbreakable crib or stroller mirrors can offer much entertainment for newborns as well. Music and scarves of contrasting colors can also help improve their senses (just remember to never leave them unsupervised with the scarf). You may even want to move their limbs to music to help them understand beats and sounds more—as long as you're gentle with them.
- *Diaper change exchange.* Deciding who should get up in the middle of the night to change the baby's diaper can be hard, especially when you and your partner are both exhausted. Taking turns can help solve this issue by deciding who will handle which nights and sticking to that schedule. Sometimes, you and your partner may have to switch it up, depending on how exhausted one of you is from the day, and that's okay. As long as the workload is distributed, you both will get through diaper changes just fine.

- *Is it normal for babies to regurgitate milk?* Yes. You may get scared when this happens, but it's entirely normal and fine for your baby to expel some milk out with their burps after feeding. Don't be alarmed when this happens. Simply clean your baby with a towel or burp cloth and move on with your day. If there are more symptoms of something else, like a fever or discomfort, consider taking your child to the pediatrician or calling the nurse for advice.
- *Bassinet vs. crib.* Many new parents will prefer a bassinet over a crib because it is smaller and easily moved. However, a crib will be large enough for your baby as they grow, whereas a bassinet will not be large enough to accommodate your baby during the toddler phase. Both are acceptable for your newborn's sleep and development. The safest option? Have both and retire the bassinet when your baby can sit up or roll over.

Baby Development: The First Year

Your pediatrician may as well be your home away from home because you may be there often. Every few months, you'll be stopping by for more vaccines, checkups, and miscellaneous issues like terrible diaper rashes or sensitive skin. In fact, within the first year, your child will have six wellness appointments at the following ages:

- Month One
- Month Two
- Month Four
- Month Six
- Month Nine
- Month Twelve

These appointments are routine, and your child's doctor will be measuring your baby's length, taking their weight, and conducting a complete physical. The pediatrician will listen to your child's heart and lungs, check their eyes, ears, and mouth, assess the soft spots on your infant's head and make sure the shape of your child's head is within normal limits, check reflexes, assess any jaundiced skin, look for rashes, and check for birthmarks, evaluate your child's belly and the umbilical cord stump, and make sure their genitals are free of any infection or rash. Pediatricians will also be looking to see if the testes for baby boys have "descended into the scrotum" (Beer, 2019). They will also make sure any circumcision procedures are healing well. Finally, the pediatrician will move your baby's hips and legs to make sure their range of motion is functional.

Any vaccinations due at that time will be administered. This may be scary because you don't want to see your child in any pain. However, these vaccines and inoculations will prevent your child from getting much more serious diseases. Usually, a parent will hold the infant while the shots are administered to give them all the love and comfort they require.

Any questions you have can be answered during the exam. Don't hesitate to voice any concerns. Remember, your child's pediatrician has probably seen everything, and you shouldn't be afraid to ask questions. Keep in mind that many pediatrician practices will have a helpline for you to call when something comes up. For example, any rashes, bumps, or concerns can have an answer in only a few minutes. The nurse or doctor at the practice can help you make the best medical decisions for your child.

Tip #10: Familiarize Yourself With Common Cold Symptoms & Other Ailments.

By making yourself more familiar with some of the common ailments that infants struggle with, you will be ready for your baby's first cold. This can be a terrifying time for you and your partner, and you will likely be able to think of nothing else when this time comes. However, be prepared by having all the proper medications, thermometers, and tools you need to help your baby get over it quicker.

12

YOUR NEW (BETTER) LIFE IS COMING

Life feels so much bigger with your baby now out of the womb and growing before your eyes. Doesn't it? Getting used to daily living with a baby in the house will be a challenge but a welcome one. Getting used to daily living with a baby in the house will be a challenge but a welcome one. You and your partner need to make adjustments to accommodate your new bundle of joy. For example, having a fully-functional diaper bag for outings and learning which foods your child likes most will be challenges that you didn't know were so hard to handle and so fulfilling. Learning how your child speaks, what makes your baby laugh, and coming home to see your baby and partner are some of the joys that your new life has to offer. Not only that, but as your child gets older and older, you and your partner can look forward to stolen moments of alone time— especially during your child's naptime.

All of these aspects of fatherhood will come together to form a cauldron of love, family, and joy that you'll harbor for a lifetime.

Leaving The House

Something as simple as a grocery store trip might feel like you're packing to go on a vacation or a hike. Or both. A fully stocked diaper bag will be your first necessity. That means it will have all of the following:

- *Diapers.* Ideally, you'll want to have eight diapers or more in your diaper bag for short grocery store runs. If you're going out for longer than a few hours, you'll likely want to have a day or two's worth of diapers. You may want to leave a backup package in your car for emergencies on the road.
- *Wipes.* One whole travel pack should suffice, but for longer trips, consider taking two packs.
- *Diaper rash cream.* Diaper rashes are no fun for anyone—baby or parent alike. Use baby powder and ointments to avoid rashes altogether, and have a small tube of diaper rash cream when the unavoidable rash pops up.
- *Baby powder.* This is a lifesaver for babies crawling and moving around more, and babies with sensitive skin or adverse reactions to baby wipes. Baby powder can help avoid chafing and irritated skin from the constant diaper movement.
- *Body lotion.* This is mostly to keep dry skin and eczema at bay. Some babies will have naturally dry skin and may need lotion to avoid any cracking from the dryness they experience.
- *Sunscreen.* The last thing you and your partner need is a sunburnt baby. Not only will they be uncomfortable, but there won't be much you can do for them besides applying a lot of aloe lotion. Put a generous amount of sunscreen on your baby before leaving the house on days where the UV is expected to be high.

- *Changes of baby clothes.* Three sets should do for short trips, but you'll need more if you're staying out longer. Also, keep in mind how your baby eats. If your baby is notoriously messy while eating or vomits a lot after a feeding, you'll want extra clothing for these instances. Some families will pack—and use—up to six outfits for small outings. There is no shame in being over-prepared.
- *A sweater, hat, and extra socks.* Even in warm weather, your baby may need a hat to protect from the sun.
- *Two swaddling blankets.* Again, babies are messy. Bringing only one is asking for disaster. Bring a backup in the case of a milk spill, vomit, or messy burp.
- *Formula or refrigerated breast milk in an insulated bag.* Either a travel-sized can of powdered formula or several small bottles of pre-made liquid concentrate will do. Either option is good for your baby. Parents who breastfeed might have an easier time feeding the baby on the go since their mother can feed them while sitting down, strolling through a store, or sitting in a parked (and off) car. However, if you are out with the baby by yourself, you'll have to prepare the breast milk in a bottle and feed your baby as usual.
- *Two clean bottles for feeding.* Having two is a good start, but longer trips may require a third bottle. Consider how long you'll be out of the house and how accessible a sink will be.
- *A set of bibs.* Usually, two or three will suffice for some trips, but you will need more depending on how messy your baby eats.
- *A changing pad.* You'll need these in those germ-ridden public restrooms or for any other inconvenient spot you may have to change your baby in, like the backseat of your car or on the ground at the park. Sometimes, a bathroom won't be available for you to use.

- *Pacifiers in a plastic case.* The case helps keep pacifiers clean and is washable.
- *Plastic ziplock bags.* There is nothing grosser than digging through your diaper bag and pulling out a hand covered in solidified milk from a dirty outfit. Keep those dirty outfits and bibs securely tucked away for the laundry pile in a ziplock bag.
- *Some of your baby's favorite toys, rattles, or entertainment accessories.* Babies get bored like the rest of us and are not easily assuaged by daytime soap operas.
- *An infant first-aid kit.* These kits have small band-aids, ointments, and other materials for small scrapes your baby may get from crawling about the yard or a relative's house.

While you will likely not need all of these things all at once, you must be ready for anything your child may need. Whether a really full diaper or a feeding, you must be ready.

Of course, there are other needs when going out. For example, you'll need your child's car seat for any drive. If you are going somewhere that requires a lot of walking, you'll probably want your child's stroller as well. Many models of car seats and infant carriers come with a matching stroller.

At times, you may feel like you're bringing everything except the kitchen sink, and that may be true a lot of the time. In the early months of your baby's life, you'll need a lot of things for even the shortest trips to see relatives. If you and your family find yourself visiting one particular relative frequently, consider leaving a stash of baby supplies at that relative's house for an easier commute.

Trying New Foods

"The Dietary Guidelines for American and the American Academy of Pediatrics recommend children be introduced to foods other than breast milk or infant formula when they are about [six] months old" ("When, What, and How," 2021).

When your baby hits the six-month mark, they will be crawling, playing more, and giggling like a maniac. You'll likely be having a great time as a father—although tired from some of the late nights as your toddler is still learning how to navigate this brand-new world.

Introducing new foods can be a fun and exciting prospect for any parent and the beginning of you truly bonding with your baby. Since your partner has likely done much of the legwork in the pregnancy and newborn stages, you can now have a hand in some of the new experiences in your toddler's expanding world. This begins with food. Your child is likely ready to try new foods if they meet the following criteria:

- "Sits up alone or with support.
- Is able to control their head and neck.
- Opens their mouth when food is offered.
- Swallows food rather than pushes it back out onto the chin.
- Brings objects to the mouth.
- Tries to grasp small objects, such as toys or food.
- Transfers food from the front of the back of the tongue to swallow" ("When, What and How," 2021).

Most children will not need foods given in any particular order, which means that you and your partner can start with whatever foods you are most interested in trying, as long as they are prepared in a way appropriate for your baby's age. This means avoiding foods that are choking hazards or contain dangerous material. For example, honey should not be introduced to your child's diet before age one as it "contains spores of a bacteria called *Clostridium botulinum*. This could possibly cause botulism—a serious condition that attacks the body's nerves, according to the Centers for Disease Control and Prevention (CDC)" (Harris, 2020). Also, always remember to check for bones in any meat or fish products.

As your child hits the seven- and eight-month mark, they should be able to eat from a variety of different food groups. Cereals, meats, fruits, and vegetables are all great food groups to start with.

You may be curious how even to start. Good question. Start with a single-food ingredient that can help your child acclimate to the change. Testing for any allergies is ideal, as well. Do this by separating the introduction of new foods by three to five days. That means you will be starting with one food for three to five days and slowly introducing another while looking for any adverse effects this food may have on your baby.

When you have introduced other foods, you may want to consider introducing "potentially allergenic foods" ("When, What, and How," 2021). These include:

- Milk products
- Eggs
- Fish and shellfish
- Tree nuts, peanuts, and sesame
- Wheat
- Soy

Although cow's milk is not recommended for children under one year, milk products like cheese and yogurts can be introduced earlier, as long as you and your partner monitor for any allergic reactions like eczema or welts.

Make preparing your child's food simple. Use pre-made, jarred options for families who lack the time or desire to make their own baby food. Baby food recipes can be easy with practice. Babies will require foods to be mashed, pureed, or strained and smooth. Your baby will likely need some time to get used to the textures of many foods and might cough, spit up, or gag on some of the foods. Stay calm when this happens and observe what they do. Start with small, easily dissolved portions. Pureed cereal, mashed potatoes, and pureed carrots are easy options for first-time parents to start with.

Consider keeping a log of your child's likes and dislikes in a digital note on your phone or a small notebook. Having this record will not only show your child how much you love and care about them but give them insight into themselves as a baby. This can be a great heirloom for any growing family.

Babbling: The Language of Babies

Babbling is one of those magical moments of fatherhood that can bring you to your knees real quick. One minute, you think you've got it all figured out, and then they start using their voice to try and talk to you. They try to imitate your sounds, have conversations with you, and communicate with you. As babies grow, they begin speaking to their parents all the time. They use their vocal cords to communicate even though they don't know words quite yet, and most of the time, you'll have no idea what it means—even though you love the sound of their delightful little sounds.

However, researcher Laura Cirelli discovered that toddlers use music and sound to create connections (Vedantam *et al.*, 2018). This means that babbling is a predictable and teachable language that you can decipher. Lullabies, songs, and singing from a baby's parents are cues that babies use to connect with other people.

Furthermore, Rachel Albert, a psychology professor who studies babbling, says that the repetitive syllables you may hear in your child's babbling are important. Simply put, these syllables mean one thing: your baby is learning. "Babbles create an opportunity for a social feedback loop—also known as conversation" (Vedantam *et al.*, 2018).

Your baby will develop their babbling over the first few years of their lives until they finally begin speaking in clear and coherent words, sentences, and phrases. Until then, you'll start to learn what several of your child's babbles mean. In time, you may notice that your child will often point to something while making a certain noise. They may be trying to imitate the words that you and your partner often use but can't seem to form the sound. Eventually, you and your partner will begin to identify what the little sounds your baby makes equate to around the house. These are often small things, like your child saying, "I'm hungry."

Remember that babies will learn at their own pace, and your child's babbling is a great sign that they are learning from their best possible role models: mom and dad.

Making Your Baby Laugh

If there was anything you learned from your partner's pregnancy, it was that babies operate on their own timeline. This applies to everything in their life—even their smiles and laughs. Your baby will laugh when they are ready, and the most you can do is encourage them by doing a bunch of things that will fill them with love and fun. Keep careful note of what does the trick because when your baby lets out that first irresistible giggle, you'll be hooked on the sound forever. Here are some things that can get your baby laughing:

- Copy their own babbling and sounds.
- Observe what your baby smiles about and reenact those instances.
- Get excited when your baby smiles and coos so they feel encouraged to continue.

- Play peek-a-boo with your baby.
- Use rattles, unbreakable mirrors, and picture books to encourage them to smile and laugh.
- Put toys near your child so that their limbs will touch them and make noise when your baby moves.
- Gentle bouncing on a lap or knee.
- Making silly noises with your mouth and tongue while touching your baby's belly or limbs.
- Funny faces are a society favorite.
- Tickling!

Remember to take everything slowly—even laughing. Some babies won't let out their first real laugh until they're three or four months old.

Returning To Work

Work is an essential part of a functioning family. It may be hard for some fathers to return to work knowing that they will be missing out on a lot of their baby's life and milestones, but providing for the family is crucial. Some families may be dual-income households, which can be even harder for some fathers to accept that their baby will be in a daycare facility all day while both parents are working.

However scary, the time to plan for work has come. Some important questions to think about as you and your partner discuss your family dynamic are:

- What daycare facility will you be using?
- Do we have a backup childcare plan for when our baby is sick or the facility is closed?
- Will your schedules match?
- How much family time will you have together, and will it be enough?

- Is there any assistance or programs that your family can take advantage of?
- Can we afford to take a few short days in the first week back?
- Who can we lean on for extra support?

When you've answered some of these questions, you can assess the current state of your situation with your partner. These questions might unnerve you, but there are things you can do to make your transition back to the workplace as smooth as possible (Knight, 2019). Some do's and don'ts to keep in mind:

Do:

- Be kind to yourself and your emotions. It's okay to call and check on your child or partner after returning to work. It's also okay to have a lot of emotions running through you. Your life has just had a dramatic shift. The first two or three weeks back at work may be the hardest, and it's important to take some time before reacting to any emotions. Allow yourself to simply *feel*.
- Practice your workday in your head. Try to visualize what a typical workday would look like. This can help you acclimate to your new schedule and life.
- Be direct with your boss. Yes, you may need to leave early some days, and emergencies may require your attention. Letting your boss know beforehand can set the expectation that you may need some special accommodations.

Don't:

- Use your first day back to work as the first day your child is in the care of someone else. This will only cause a lot of stress and anxiety. Instead, practice this a few times before you and your partner leave your child in another person's care for work. This will help smooth out the anxieties of that first day at work.

- Remain silent when you need some flexibility in the workplace. You'll need more support, and plenty of workplace programs exist to help new parents adjust to their new lives. Consider speaking with your boss or HR department about programs your workplace offers for childcare, assistance, or discount rates on neighboring facilities.
- Assume you'll be able to function the same as you had before your child was born. You may assume your professional life might remain just as strong as it had been before you welcomed your baby into the world, but it might not. You may not be as willing to take on extra shifts, more hours, or added projects because you want to go home and see your baby. There is nothing wrong with this, and, in time, you'll get your professional edge back.

Sex After A Baby

It's okay to recognize that you and your partner both have needs. You, obviously, will be ready for sex much sooner than your partner —who, you know, just had a baby. There will be several weeks or months in which you and your partner may forgo intimacy due to exhaustion and fear. However, there are some ways to get through the drought.

The first thing to realize is that your sex life with your partner will come back and that it will likely be better than ever. In the meantime, here are some tips to keep in mind:

- Take cues from your partner. She's the one who birthed your child. She may be healing for a while, physically and emotionally. Traumatic births can have women feeling scared and anxious about getting intimate again. Let her take the lead with your sex life, and clearly tell her that you are doing so.

- Practice patience. It may be frustrating to wait, but you can help by asking your partner what you can do to support her healing process. This support and love can make your partner feel emotionally connected to you again, as well.
- Recognize which feelings you are having. Sometimes, you may not be feeling it just as much as she isn't, and that might confuse you. It's okay to be disinterested or confused.
- Pique her interest by helping out around the house and complimenting her. This can help her feel like you're invested in your household and want what's best for her. Sometimes, that notion isn't as obvious as we think it is.
- Keep the lines of communication open. If you're feeling something, it's okay to tell your partner about these feelings, as long as you're gentle and considerate of her own. As long as you and your partner maintain healthy communication, your relationship is in good hands.

By simply being there for your partner, you're more likely to revive her interest in sex. Having patience and offering your support can be everything that you both need to find your sex life among the adjustments of your new life.

Tip #11: Learn How To Cope With Change

Some people may struggle with the new direction their lives have taken. It's entirely normal for you to feel afraid, depressed, or nervous about the direction your life is going in. Consider starting a journal to record your feelings and discuss your emotions with a mental health professional. In time, you'll accept that your previous way of life has morphed, and you can now build the foundations for a new one going forward.

CONCLUSION

Fatherhood is not a sprint but a marathon. It's a hike through the Amazon Rainforest with a backpack full of equipment you aren't sure how to use. This journey from conception to birth and beyond will be one that will build the foundations for the rest of your life. The adventure you and your partner have embarked on will be rife with ups and downs, trial and error, and a hundred small things that might make you want to rip your hair out.

However, it'll all be worth it. With every baby giggle, every smile, the first time they say "daddy," and their first steps, you'll feel like you've been shown a side of the world you hadn't known existed.

Throughout your partner's pregnancy, you have watched your child grow and morph from a small, half-ounce fetus into a several-pound baby who now rests in your arms. Their every coo and cry will be etched into your memory forever.

You have learned dozens of tips, techniques, and information from men who became fathers before you by reading this book. You have learned from their mistakes and will walk a new path completely different than theirs, although you have one common attribute: you are all fathers.

Within these pages, you've learned how your child grew within their mother's womb, at what point their organs formed, and when they'll be able to hear your voice. You've learned how to pack a diaper bag, when to go with your partner to the hospital, and how to hold your newborn baby. You've learned about the patience you will need during your fatherhood journey and how hard it may feel sometimes, but it's worth it.

You may look at yourself in the mirror while you hold your infant child and think about how different you are and how much you have changed since that first decision to have a child. This growth will continue as you watch your child become an adult. Congratulations and good luck with your new life.

REFERENCES

101 things soon-to-be dads need to know about pregnancy, birth, postpartum, and being a new dad. hiccapop. (n.d.). Retrieved November 9, 2021, from https://www.hiccapop.com/blogs/blog/101-things-soon-to-be-dads-need-to-know-about-pregnancy-birth-postpartum-and-being-a-new-dad.

Abramson, A. (2019, December 13). *10 pieces of advice financial planners give to new parents who don't know where to start.* Business Insider. Retrieved November 9, 2021, from https://www.businessinsider.com/personal-finance/advice-financial-planners-give-to-new-parents.

Antenatal classes. Pregnancy Birth and Baby. (n.d.). Retrieved November 9, 2021, from https://www.pregnancybirthbaby.org.au/antenatal-classes.

Ayuda, T. (n.d.). *What to expect from your third trimester prenatal appointment.* BabyCenter. Retrieved November 9, 2021, from https://www.babycenter.com/pregnancy/health-and-safety/third-trimester-prenatal-visits_9346.

Baby's first bowel movements. HealthyChildren.org. (n.d.). Retrieved November 9, 2021, from https://www.healthychildren.org/English/ages-stages/baby/diapers-clothing/Pages/Babys-First-Bowel-Movements.aspx.

Baby's first laugh: How to get your infant to giggle. Baby's First Laugh: How To Get Your Infant To Giggle. (n.d.). Retrieved November 9, 2021, from https://www.colgate.com/en-us/oral-health/infant-oral-care/babys-first-laugh-how-to-get-your-infant-to-giggle.

Bassinet vs. Crib: What's the difference and which one is best for you. Newton Baby. (n.d.). Retrieved November 9, 2021, from https://www.newtonbaby.com/blogs/nursery/bassinet-vs-crib.

Becoming a dad: Advice for expectant fathers. ZERO TO THREE. (n.d.). Retrieved November 9, 2021, from https://www.zerotothree.org/resources/1838-becoming-a-dad-advice-for-expectant-fathers.

Bell, B. (2020, August 27). *What pain meds are safe to take while pregnant?* The Checkup. Retrieved November 9, 2021, from https://www.singlecare.com/blog/pain-medicine-while-pregnant/.

Brennan, D. (2021, March 12). *3 signs you may be having precipitous Labor.* WebMD. Retrieved November 9, 2021, from https://www.webmd.com/parenting/what-is-precipitous-labor.

Brown, S. (2020, November 2). *Siied Brown says "being a father means laying down your life forever for your children.": Dear fathers.* Dear Fathers | The Premiere Media Platform for Black Fatherhood. Retrieved November 9, 2021, from https://dearfathers.com/2020/11/siied-brown/.

Cafasso, J. (2016, May 26). *Complications during pregnancy and delivery.* Healthline. Retrieved November 9, 2021, from https://www.healthline.com/health/pregnancy/delivery-complications.

Centers for Disease Control and Prevention. (2021, August 10). *Frequently asked questions (faqs)*. Centers for Disease Control and Prevention. Retrieved November 9, 2021, from https://www.cdc.gov/breastfeeding/faq/index.htm.

Centers for Disease Control and Prevention. (2021, August 24). *When, what, and how to introduce Solid Foods*. Centers for Disease Control and Prevention. Retrieved November 9, 2021, from https://www.cdc.gov/nutrition/infantandtoddlernutrition/foods-and-drinks/when-to-introduce-solid-foods.html.

Chesney, E. (2020, December 9). *When I was pregnant with my first child, my husband and I quickly decided that we wouldn't find out the gender. I just didn't want to know*. The Mabelhood. Retrieved November 9, 2021, from https://mabelslabels.com/blog/2018/11/30/10-reasons-why-not-finding-out-the-sex-of-your-baby-is-awesome/.

Cleveland Clinic. (2021, August 20). *6 ways to make your baby tired*. Cleveland Clinic. Retrieved November 9, 2021, from https://health.clevelandclinic.org/the-6-best-ways-to-make-your-baby-tired-and-3-things-not-to-do/.

Common tests during pregnancy. Johns Hopkins Medicine. (n.d.). Retrieved November 9, 2021, from https://www.hopkinsmedicine.org/health/wellness-and-prevention/common-tests-during-pregnancy.

Doheny, K. (2014, December 17). *Expectant Dads may also have hormonal changes, study suggests*. WebMD. Retrieved November 9, 2021, from https://www.webmd.com/men/news/20141217/expectant-dads-may-also-have-hormonal-changes-study-suggests.

Doucleff, M. (2019, July 15). *Sleep training truths: What science can (and can't) tell us about crying it out*. NPR. Retrieved November 9, 2021, from https://www.npr.org/sections/health-shots/2019/07/15/730339536/sleep-training-truths-what-science-can-and-cant-tell-us-about-crying-it-out.

Dubinsky, D. (n.d.). *Doctor visits for your baby's first year.* BabyCenter. Retrieved November 9, 2021, from https://www.babycenter.com/health/doctor-visits-and-vaccines/doctor-visits-for-your-babys-first-year_66.

Fetal development: Month-by-month stages of pregnancy. Cleveland Clinic. (n.d.). Retrieved November 9, 2021, from https://my.clevelandclinic.org/health/articles/7247-fetal-development-stages-of-growth.

Fields, L. (2011, May 13). *Pets and the new baby: What's safe, how to prepare.* WebMD. Retrieved November 9, 2021, from https://pets.webmd.com/features/pets-and-new-baby#2.

First trimester: Tips for dads to be. NCT (National Childbirth Trust). (2019, June 12). Retrieved November 9, 2021, from https://www.nct.org.uk/pregnancy/dads-be/first-trimester-tips-for-dads-be.

Frost, A. (2020, April 21). *Do babies cry in the womb? plus, what it may mean.* Healthline. Retrieved November 9, 2021, from https://www.healthline.com/health/pregnancy/do-babies-cry-in-the-womb.

Gavin, M. L. (Ed.). (2019, July). *Learning, play, and your newborn (for parents) - nemours kidshealth.* KidsHealth. Retrieved November 9, 2021, from https://kidshealth.org/en/parents/learnnewborn.html.

Griffin, J. (n.d.). *10 most commonly offered employee benefits.* JP Griffin Group | Employee Benefits Broker. Retrieved November 9, 2021, from https://www.griffinbenefits.com/blog/10-commonly-offered-employee-benefits.

Harris, N. (n.d.). *Why can't babies have honey?* Parents. Retrieved November 9, 2021, from https://www.parents.com/baby/feeding/when-can-my-baby-eat-honey/.

Holland, K. (2021, September 23). *Pregnancy symptoms: Early signs you may be pregnant*. Healthline. Retrieved November 9, 2021, from https://www.healthline.com/health/pregnancy/early-symptoms-timeline.

Hospital bag for dad: The ultimate checklist for what to pack. Itzy Ritzy. (n.d.). Retrieved November 9, 2021, from https://www.itzyritzy.com/blogs/news/what-to-pack-in-dads-hospital-bag.

How to hold a newborn: In pictures. Raising Children Network. (2020, May 1). Retrieved November 9, 2021, from https://raisingchildren.net.au/newborns/health-daily-care/holding-newborns/how-to-hold-your-newborn.

How to make your baby laugh. bounty.com. (2021, March 15). Retrieved November 9, 2021, from https://www.bounty.com/baby-0-to-12-months/development/how-to-make-a-baby-laugh.

How to swaddle a baby. Enfamil. (n.d.). Retrieved November 9, 2021, from https://www.enfamil.com/articles/how-to-swaddle-a-baby/.

The importance of skin-to-skin with baby after delivery. Sanford Health News. (2018, August 9). Retrieved November 9, 2021, from https://news.sanfordhealth.org/childrens/the-importance-of-skin-to-skin-after-delivery-you-should-know/.

Infertility. Infertility | Office on Women's Health. (n.d.). Retrieved November 9, 2021, from https://www.womenshealth.gov/a-z-topics/infertility.

Jeremiah. (2020, March 10). *First 20 things to do when you are going to be a dad*. Not A Power Couple. Retrieved November 9, 2021, from https://notapowercouple.com/first-20-things-to-do-new-dad/.

Johnson, T. C. (2020, August 29). *1 to 3 months pregnant - 1st Trimester Baby Growth & Development*. WebMD. Retrieved November 9, 2021, from https://www.webmd.com/baby/1to3-months.

Johnson, T. C. (2020, August 29). *4 to 6 months pregnant - 2nd Trimester Baby Growth & Development*. WebMD. Retrieved November 9, 2021, from https://www.webmd.com/baby/4to6-months.

Johnson, T. C. (2021, August 9). *7 to 9 months pregnant - 3rd trimester baby growth & development*. WebMD. Retrieved November 9, 2021, from https://www.webmd.com/baby/pregnancy-your-babys-growth-development-months-7-to-9.

Knight, R. (2021, August 31). *8 tips for returning to work after parental leave*. Harvard Business Review. Retrieved November 9, 2021, from https://hbr.org/2019/08/how-to-return-to-work-after-taking-parental-leave.

Lanter, A. (2021, September 8). *Top 10 nursery do's and don'ts*. Hello Gorgeous, by Angela Lanter. Retrieved November 9, 2021, from https://angelalanter.com/2018/08/top-10-nursery-dos-and-donts/.

Marcin, A. (2018, December 6). *When is the best time to announce pregnancy?* Healthline. Retrieved November 9, 2021, from https://www.healthline.com/health/pregnancy/when-to-announce-your-pregnancy.

Mayo Foundation for Medical Education and Research. (2020, December 18). *Ectopic pregnancy*. Mayo Clinic. Retrieved November 9, 2021, from https://www.mayoclinic.org/diseases-conditions/ectopic-pregnancy/symptoms-causes/syc-20372088.

Mayo Foundation for Medical Education and Research. (2020, January 21). *Video: Baby's soft spots (fontanels)*. Mayo Clinic. Retrieved November 9, 2021, from https://www.mayoclinic.org/healthy-lifestyle/infant-and-toddler-health/multimedia/babys-soft-spots/vid-20084737.

Mayo Foundation for Medical Education and Research. (2020, July 31). *Sex during pregnancy: What's ok, what's not*. Mayo Clinic.

Retrieved November 9, 2021, from https://www.mayoclinic.org/healthy-lifestyle/pregnancy-week-by-week/in-depth/sex-during-pregnancy/art-20045318.

Mayo Foundation for Medical Education and Research. (2021, April 14). *Premature birth.* Mayo Clinic. Retrieved November 9, 2021, from https://www.mayoclinic.org/diseases-conditions/premature-birth/symptoms-causes/syc-20376730.

McTigue, S. (2020, February 21). *Getting your baby (or toddler) to sleep in the crib: Tips and tricks.* Healthline. Retrieved November 9, 2021, from https://www.healthline.com/health/baby/baby-wont-sleep-in-crib#crib-tips-for-baby.

Napolitano, C., & Randall, S. (n.d.). *50 things every guy should know about pregnancy and parenthood.* Parents. Retrieved November 9, 2021, from https://www.parents.com/parenting/dads/101/50-things-every-guy-should-know-about-pregnancy-and-parenthood/.

The Nemours Foundation. (2018, June). *Bringing your baby home (for parents) - nemours kidshealth.* KidsHealth. Retrieved November 9, 2021, from https://kidshealth.org/en/parents/bringing-baby-home.html.

Partner support during pregnancy. Partner Support During Pregnancy | CS Mott Children's Hospital | Michigan Medicine. (n.d.). Retrieved November 9, 2021, from https://www.mottchildren.org/health-library/abp7352.

Pathak, N. (2021, March 19). *What to do when baby is overdue.* WebMD. Retrieved November 9, 2021, from https://www.webmd.com/baby/what-do-baby-overdue.

Raypole, C. (2020, March 31). *Repressed emotions: Finding and releasing them.* Healthline. Retrieved November 9, 2021, from https://www.healthline.com/health/repressed-emotions.

Robock, K. (2016, August 19). *How to safely warm a bottle of breast milk or formula*. Today's Parent. Retrieved November 9, 2021, from https://www.todaysparent.com/baby/how-to-safely-warm-a-bottle-of-breast-milk-or-formula/.

Taylor, N. (2021, May 29). *Tips for new dads: 33 tips that are great advice for expectant fathers*. Fathercraft. Retrieved November 9, 2021, from https://fathercraft.com/new-dad-tips/.

Teeth development in children. Teeth development in children - Better Health Channel. (n.d.). Retrieved November 9, 2021, from https://www.betterhealth.vic.gov.au/health/conditionsandtreatments/teeth-development-in-children.

Vedantam, S., Shah, P., Boyle, T., Kwerel, L., Frame, K., & Arcuri, B. (2018, May 14). *Baby talk: Decoding the secret language of babies*. WBUR. Retrieved November 9, 2021, from https://www.wbur.org/npr/610796636/baby-talk-decoding-the-secret-language-of-babies.

Villano, M. (n.d.). *A dad's guide to sex after baby*. Parents. Retrieved November 9, 2021, from https://www.parents.com/parenting/relationships/sex-and-marriage-after-baby/a-dads-guide-to-sex-after-pregnancy-and/.

Weiss, R. E. (2021, June 14). *Tests and exams you will need to take at prenatal care appointments*. Verywell Family. Retrieved November 9, 2021, from https://www.verywellfamily.com/what-happens-at-prenatal-care-appointments-2759791.

Weiss, R. E. (2021, September 13). *How to tell when it's time to go to the hospital for Labor*. Verywell Family. Retrieved November 9, 2021, from https://www.verywellfamily.com/when-should-i-go-to-the-hospital-to-have-my-baby-2759045.

Weiss, R. E. (2021, September 13). *Why some parents choose not to know the sex of their baby before birth*. Verywell Family. Retrieved

November 9, 2021, from https://www.verywellfamily.com/reasons-to-not-find-out-the-sex-of-your-baby-2758975.

Image Credit: Shutterstock.com

Made in the USA
Las Vegas, NV
02 June 2022

49692267R00066